www.ingramcontent.com/pod-product-compliance
Lightning Source LLC
Chambersburg PA
CBHW081218230426
43666CB00015B/2780

TEACHER'S EDITION

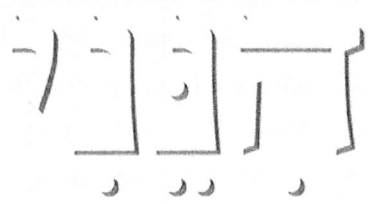

THE NEW
HEBREW THROUGH PRAYER

3

Roberta Osser Baum

Consultant:
Rabbi Martin Cohen

Behrman House, Inc.

Book and Cover Design: Itzhack Shelomi
Project Editor: Terry S. Kaye
Special Needs Education Consultant:
Sara Rubinow Simon

Copyright © 2003 Behrman House, Inc.
Springfield, New Jersey
www.behrmanhouse.com
ISBN 0-87441-135-1

CONTENTS

I. **INTRODUCTION AND OVERVIEW** — 4
   - Preface 4
   - Using This Teacher's Edition 4
   - Overview of Lesson Planning 5
   - Reinforcing Prayer Awareness 5
   - Teaching Aids 5
   - Developing Reading Skills 6
   - Classroom Games 9

II. **USING THE TEXTBOOK** — 12
   - Introducing the Textbook 12
   - Lesson 1 ..... אֵין כָּמוֹךָ\אַב הָרַחֲמִים 13
   - Lesson 2 ..... כִּי מִצִּיּוֹן\לְךָ יְיָ 25
   - Lesson 3 ..... בִּרְכוֹת הַתּוֹרָה 37
   - Lesson 4 ..... בִּרְכוֹת הַהַפְטָרָה 51
   - Lesson 5 ..... וְזֹאת הַתּוֹרָה\עֵץ חַיִּים הִיא\עַל שְׁלֹשָׁה דְבָרִים 63
   - Lesson 6 ..... עָלֵינוּ 79
   - Lesson 7 ..... קַדִּישׁ 89
   - Lesson 8 ..... אֵין כֵּאלֹהֵינוּ 101
   - Lesson 9 ..... הַשְׁכִּיבֵנוּ\שְׁמַע\מוֹדָה אֲנִי 111

III. **ENRICHMENT AND SUPPLEMENTARY MATERIALS** — 123
   - Family Education 123
   - Techniques for Use with Special Needs Students 133
   - Answers to Worksheets 134

I. INTRODUCTION AND OVERVIEW

PREFACE

You are about to embark on a sacred task, the task of teaching our children how to worship, to pray in the Hebrew language. In doing so, you will help them connect with our God, with our ancestors, and with our heritage.

As Jewish educators, we want to help our students develop positive attitudes toward our rich Jewish tradition. Toward this end, *Hineni—The New Hebrew Through Prayer* is designed to deepen our students' understanding of Jewish ritual and the concepts inherent in our mitzvot, while teaching them to read Hebrew and to pray. The prayer selections introducing each lesson encourage participation in the rituals of synagogue and home. And the enrichment activities aid students in developing reading fluency, allowing for active participation in the classroom setting. This approach encourages students to feel comfortable in their learning environment, where they sharpen their reading skills and develop a familiarity and understanding of rituals and mitzvot.

USING THIS TEACHER'S EDITION

This Teacher's Edition contains the entire text of *Hineni—The New Hebrew Through Prayer 3*, reproduced in reduced size. The pages are annotated with suggested activities, teaching methods, and other information to assist you. Black-line masters that supplement the material are also provided in this Teacher's Edition.

Keep in mind that students learn in different ways, and any student's primary learning mode may be aural, visual, or tactile. Similarly, teachers teach in different ways. Don't feel obligated to use a method that does not feel comfortable with your teaching style. By the same token, remember that since students learn in different ways, you should vary your teaching methods accordingly. Feel free to repeat an activity or method that worked especially well for you and your students.

> The information and suggestions in this Teacher's Edition are intended to assist you in developing your own teaching plan. You do not need to follow every suggestion on every page. Rather, the guide provides you with many different options from which to choose.

Pacing

Students differ in ability. Teachers differ in style. Schools differ in the number of class sessions scheduled each week. Ultimately, you must decide how to pace your class through the text.

The lessons in *Hineni* vary in length. Some lessons may take three or more sessions, while others will take one or two. A short but more difficult lesson may take more time to teach than a longer, simpler lesson.

Homework

Whether or not to give homework is a question that should be addressed to your school principal. Keep in mind that homework can provide students with the additional contact, repetition, and reinforcement of what has already been learned in class. Homework should not be used as a tool to teach new information.

If you do give homework, *Hineni* makes assigning homework easy. At the end of each lesson in the Teacher's Edition is a review worksheet. These review worksheets can be duplicated and completed for homework, or, of course, they can be used for in-class evaluation.

Be sure to review each homework assignment during the class session following the assignment. Doing this reinforces the importance of the homework and reassures the students that their efforts were noted and were a worthwhile expenditure of time.

Family Education

A partnership between home and school can help your students reach their greatest potential in their Hebrew studies. Parents can be important allies in the education of your students, and every effort should be made to facilitate this partnership. To aid you in this endeavor, black-line masters to duplicate and send home for the family are included in this Teacher's Edition.

OVERVIEW OF LESSON PLANNING

Timing is an important factor in planning your classes. Keep in mind the objectives of the program as you plan your lesson for the day. Foremost in your mind should be not how quickly you move through the text, but rather how effectively you teach the material and how thoroughly the students master it. Remember that review and reinforcement are essential ingredients for mastery.

There are nine lessons in *Hineni 3*. How you pace your class should depend on the number of classroom sessions each week, your students' reading ability, and the length of the particular passages. It is important to decide beforehand which activities you will cover in each session and how much time you will allot to each activity. Make sure that reading is a part of *every* lesson. The materials in the textbook and in this Teacher's Edition, as well as teacher reinforcement through games and Word Card work, should all come into play to ensure the success of the program.

REINFORCING PRAYER AWARENESS

Developing comfort and familiarity with the prayers on the part of your students is an important aspect of your goal. Several strategies can help you to achieve this objective.

Prayer Service

Begin each class with a short (two- to five-minute) prayer service, including the prayers learned to date. Ask individual students to take turns as leaders.

You may choose to end the service by having the class recite this blessing.

בָּרוּךְ אַתָּה, יְיָ אֱלֹהֵינוּ, מֶלֶךְ הָעוֹלָם,
אֲשֶׁר קִדְּשָׁנוּ בְּמִצְוֹתָיו וְצִוָּנוּ לַעֲסוֹק
בְּדִבְרֵי תוֹרָה.

Praised are You, Adonai our God, Ruler of the universe, who has made us holy with commandments and commands us to engage in the study of Torah.

Create Your Own Prayerbook

After learning each prayer, you may ask students to write the prayer and its English meaning in a personal prayerbook. Students may wish to write the prayers in calligraphy (see below) and illustrate or illuminate their work. These prayerbooks can then be used at every class prayer service.

Calligraphy

Most lessons offer an opportunity for students to practice Hebrew calligraphy. This can be done on a variety of levels: simple printing, copying a text, or learning formal calligraphy as practiced by a *sofer* (scribe).

Students can use any writing medium, but we recommend investing in felt-tip pens specifically designed for calligraphy. They are inexpensive, and the results justify the expenditure.

You may wish to exhibit students' efforts on bulletin boards and in other displays.

TEACHING AIDS

Chalkboard

Use the chalkboard to introduce new words and prayers, to answer questions, to play games, and to present assignments.

Remember to vary the way in which you use the chalkboard. This can be as simple as changing the chalk color or varying the size of the letters you write.

Draw a picture on the chalkboard to illustrate the lesson. (The less polished an artist you are, the more the class will love your drawings.)

Incorporate children's need for physical movement. Plan quick-paced exercises that involve coming to the board. For example, have students copy a word that you have written on the board. There is really nothing more special about writing on a chalkboard than on paper—unless you are a child. Coming to the front of the room and writing on the board is exciting to many students. If they enjoy using the board, let them do so.

Flannelboard

A flannelboard can be used with the entire class, with small groups, or by a single student. It saves writing time at the chalkboard and presents letters and words exactly as they appear in a printed book. It also offers students the opportunity to manipulate words to form whole phrases.

Flannelboards can be purchased at a school supplies store or may be easily constructed by covering a large piece of cardboard with flannel. You can make flannelboard words by gluing a small piece of velcro or sandpaper onto the back of existing Word Cards or by cutting flashcards out of rough-textured construction paper. Most flannelboard techniques will also work with a magnetic board.

The flannelboard can be used to introduce new words and display them clearly. It is also useful for drill or review.

DEVELOPING READING SKILLS

Alef-Bet Review

Begin the year with a thorough review of the letters and vowels in the Hebrew alphabet. Use an *alef-bet* poster, *alef-bet* flashcards, or the Word Cards for *Hineni 1 or 2*. You can also use a transitional reading text such as the *Back-to-School Hebrew Reading Refresher* to review and drill Hebrew decoding before students begin *Hineni 3*.

Stopwatch and Tape Recorder

A stopwatch is an easy way to assess improvement in reading fluency. It can be used to time the speed at which a student reads a passage. Many students enjoy the experience of competing against and trying to improve their own best time.

A tape recorder also provides students with tangible evidence of their improvement. Record members of the class as they read a passage. Remember the order in which they have read. Two or three weeks later, record the students, in the same order, while they read the passage on a second tape, then play back both and compare.

Word Cards

There is a set of Word Cards available for use with *Hineni 3*. These cards, printed on durable, heavy cardboard, include all key words covered by the book. (Each Word Card is numbered for easy reference to activities included in this Teacher's Edition.) The English meaning is on the back of each Word Card.

Word Cards may be used by individuals or small groups of students, or by the class as a whole. Activities should be both teacher and student initiated, to reinforce reading skills. Possible games and teaching strategies using Word Cards are endless, and each teacher will develop many ways of using them. The following suggestions may be implemented as presented here or adapted as necessary.

Remember to use the Word Cards regularly and with a variety of techniques.

General Word Card Techniques and Games

1. Display a number of Word Cards on the edge of the chalkboard or in a pocket chart. Provide a clue about one of the words and ask the students to read the correct word. For example, "This is the Jewish state"—*Yisrael*.

2. Distribute Word Cards to the class. Call out, one at a time, the Hebrew words and phrases found on the individual cards. Ask the student with the matching card to supply the correct answer by standing up, displaying the card, and reading the word or phrase.

3. Make a packet of ten Word Cards. Arrange the class in a circle (sitting or standing) and have the students pass the packet around the circle while playing music on a tape or CD player. (Try to use Jewish or Israeli music.) When the music stops, the student holding the packet should read and/or translate the top card. This card is then placed at the bottom of the pile and the game continues in the same fashion.

4. Create two rows of Word Cards with six cards in each row. Ask students individually (or in two teams) to choose a row. Taking turns, ask the individual students or teams to read the six Hebrew words, then switch and read the words in the other row. You can also play the game by translating the words instead of reading them.

5. Post at least six words in a column on the board. Ask individuals or teams to take turns "climbing up the ladder" by reading and translating the words in the column in ascending order. Score one point for each word read correctly and two points for each word translated correctly. Then play again by having students read the words in descending order to climb down the ladder.

6. Place Word Cards on the edge of the chalkboard in full view of the class. Read the words one at a time, calling on students to go to the board and remove the identified card. Variation: Have one of the students read the words.

7. You can play a memory game with double sets of Word Cards (two identical cards for each word). Lay out eight pairs of words (sixteen cards in all) upside down and shuffled, in rows. Call on a student to pick a card and read it aloud, then try to find its match. If successful, the student must then tell the meaning of the word in order to keep the pair. On successfully giving the meaning, the student keeps the cards and two new cards are put down. If the student is unsuccessful, then the initial cards are returned to their place face down. Then the next student goes.

Pronunciation and Translation

1. Show a card and ask for volunteers to read.
2. Show a card and read together with the class.
3. Lightning Review: Show a card to one student, who has 5–10 seconds to pronounce the word; immediately show the next card to another student until everyone has participated.
4. Ask students to drill each other.

Reinforcing Word Order

1. Place cards on a flannelboard in the correct order; have students read the prayer (as a group and individually).
2. Ask students to close their eyes; remove one or more cards. Ask which words are missing.
3. Scramble all the cards for the words in a prayer. Ask students to place the cards in the correct order.
4. Scramble all the cards for the words in a prayer and put one or more aside. Ask students to place cards in the correct order and determine what is missing.
5. Distribute all the cards in a prayer, one per student. Ask students to come to the front of the room and stand in the order of the words of the prayer.
6. Distribute all the cards in a prayer, one per student, plus extra words not from the prayer. Proceed as in step 5 above, but ask students holding the extra words to step aside.

Word Cards

The following is a list of words included in *Hineni 3*:

1.	אֵין	(there is) none		51.	שָׁלוֹם	peace
2.	כָּמוֹךָ	like you		52.	עַל	on
3.	(כְּ)מַעֲשֶׂיךָ	(like) your deeds		53.	שְׁלֹשָׁה	three
4.	מַלְכוּתְךָ	your sovereignty		54.	דְּבָרִים	things
5.	וּמֶמְשַׁלְתְּךָ	and your reign		55.	הָעוֹלָם	the world
6.	מֶלֶךְ	(is) ruler		56.	עוֹמֵד	stands
7.	מָלָךְ	ruled		57.	הַתּוֹרָה	the Torah
8.	יִמְלֹךְ	will rule		58.	הָעֲבוֹדָה	the worship
9.	הָרַחֲמִים	merciful, the mercy		59.	גְּמִילוּת חֲסָדִים	acts of loving-kindness
10.	יְרוּשָׁלַיִם	Jerusalem		60.	עָלֵינוּ	it is our duty
11.	בָּטַחְנוּ	we trust(ed)		61.	לְשַׁבֵּחַ	to praise
12.	מִצִּיּוֹן	from Zion		62.	(לְ)אָדוֹן	God
13.	תּוֹרָה	Torah, teaching		63.	הַכֹּל	of all
14.	וּדְבַר	and the word of		64.	וַאֲנַחְנוּ	and we
15.	מִירוּשָׁלַיִם	from Jerusalem		65.	וּמוֹדִים	and thank
16.	שֶׁנָּתַן	who gave		66.	מֶלֶךְ מַלְכֵי הַמְּלָכִים	Ruler of rulers
17.	לְעַמּוֹ	to God's people		67.	הָאָרֶץ	the land
18.	בִּקְדֻשָּׁתוֹ	in God's holiness		68.	בַּיּוֹם הַהוּא	on that day
19.	בָּחַר	chose (choosing)		69.	יִהְיֶה	will be
20.	בָּנוּ	us		70.	קָדִישׁ	holy
21.	מִכָּל	from all		71.	יִתְגַּדַּל	will be great
22.	הָעַמִּים	the nations		72.	וְיִתְקַדַּשׁ	and will be holy
23.	וְנָתַן	and gave (and giving)		73.	שְׁמֵהּ	God's name
24.	לָנוּ	to us		74.	בְּעָלְמָא	in the world
25.	תּוֹרָתוֹ	God's Torah		75.	וְיַמְלִיךְ	and will rule
26.	נוֹתֵן	gives		76.	מַלְכוּתֵהּ	God's kingdom
27.	תּוֹרַת	Torah of		77.	וּבְחַיֵּי	and in the life of
28.	אֱמֶת	truth		78.	לְעָלַם	forever
29.	וְחַיֵּי	and life (of)		79.	וְיִשְׁתַּבַּח	and will be praised
30.	עוֹלָם	eternal, world		80.	בְּרִיךְ	blessed
31.	(בִּ)נְבִיאִים	prophets		81.	בִּרְכָתָא	blessing
32.	טוֹבִים	good (faithful)		82.	שְׁלָמָא	peace
33.	הַנֶּאֱמָרִים	spoken		83.	אֵין כּ	there is none like
34.	בֶּאֱמֶת	in truth		84.	מִי כ	who is like
35.	הַבּוֹחֵר	the one who chooses		85.	נוֹדֶה ל	we will give thanks to
36.	עַבְדּוֹ	God's servant		86.	אַתָּה הוּא	you are
37.	עַמּוֹ	God's people		87.	אֱלֹהֵינוּ	our God
38.	וְצֶדֶק	and righteousness (justice)		88.	אֲדוֹנֵינוּ	our sovereign
39.	וְזֹאת	and this is		89.	מַלְכֵּנוּ	our ruler
40.	שָׂם	placed, put		90.	מוֹשִׁיעֵנוּ	our savior
41.	מֹשֶׁה	Moses		91.	הַשְׁכִּיבֵנוּ	make us lie down
42.	לִפְנֵי	before		92.	וְהַעֲמִידֵנוּ	and make us stand up
43.	בְּנֵי	people of		93.	סֻכַּת	the shelter of
44.	יִשְׂרָאֵל	Israel		94.	שְׁלוֹמֶךָ	your peace
45.	עֵץ	tree		95.	מוֹדֶה\מוֹדָה	give thanks
46.	חַיִּים	(of) life		96.	אֲנִי	I
47.	מְאֻשָּׁר	happy		97.	לְפָנֶיךָ	to you (before you)
48.	דְּרָכֶיהָ	its ways		98.	חַי	living
49.	דַּרְכֵי	ways of		99.	וְקַיָּם	and everlasting
50.	נֹעַם	pleasantness				

CLASSROOM GAMES

Games can add variety and interest to a lesson. They reinforce learning through a medium that quickly catches the students' attention. As you plan to use the games found below, or others you develop on your own, keep the following considerations in mind:

1. Use games that move quickly.
2. Stop when students' interest begins to lag.
3. Choose games appropriate to the age group.
4. When playing a game with the entire class, see that all students become actively involved.
5. Choose games that contribute to improving specific skills and reading fluency.
6. Use games that are easy to follow and organize. Explain rules clearly. Avoid complicated directions. You want students' attention focused on the skills being reinforced, not on rules.
7. Maintain control of the class.

What's Missing?

Decide on a set of lines in a prayer passage from which to draw words. Divide the class into two teams, then choose a word and write it without vowels in two different places on the chalkboard. Each team (with members playing individually, one at a time, or as a group) must locate the word in the set of lines, go to the board and, using the book for reference, add the vowels. The first team to do so then gets the chance to read the word correctly (from either the board or the book), and if correct, they score a point. If incorrect, then the other team (having located the word and written in the vowels) gets a chance to read and score a point.

Word Search

This game will help students recognize phrases within a prayer passage. Each student has a pencil, paper, and text open to a prayer passage. (The teacher might choose to focus the students' attention on a given set of lines within the passage.) The class is divided into two teams. The teacher reads a word aloud. Students search for the word and write it down, along with the word immediately following it, to complete a phrase. (A word is often found more than once in a prayer passage; therefore, more than one answer is possible.) Students are given a specified amount of time to search for the word and write the phrase. The teacher calls "Stop" and pencils are put down. A point is given for each team member who found and wrote the phrase in the allotted time.

Variation: Instead of writing the phrase, the teacher calls out the first word in a phrase, then the two team players search for the word and race to the chalkboard (or any other "target"). The first to hit the "target" reads the phrase and earns a point for the team.

Speed Reading

Individual Competition

Using a watch with a second hand, or a stopwatch, time individual students reading an assigned set of lines three separate times. The goal is for the students to improve their previous record. If the student reads a word incorrectly, ask the student to repeat the word correctly in order to proceed. Allow each student a maximum time of 60 seconds before proceeding to the next student. You may also allow students their own choice of lines to read.

Teams

Divide the class into two teams—Team A and Team B. Select a prayer passage (or set of lines) for students to read. Ask each student on Team A to read a word or line in turn until the passage is completed, while timing the team. Then ask Team B to try to achieve a better time while reading the same selection in the same manner. Then reverse, using a different prayer passage or set of lines, with Team B going first. If a reader makes a mistake, ask him or her to read the word correctly before proceeding. (Alternative: When a word is read incorrectly, the word should be "passed along" to the next student who finishes the first student's word[s] and then continues with his or her own.)

Class

Announce a target time—a period of time for the class to beat while reading a particular prayer passage or set of lines. Ask each student to read one word in turn. If the class beats the target time, ask them to repeat the activity and try to beat the new time.

Tic-Tac-Toe

Draw a Tic-Tac-Toe diagram on the chalkboard. Divide students into two teams, X and O. Show a Word Card, then call on a student from Team X to read the Hebrew word. If the student reads correctly, ask him or her to place an X in one of the squares. Then it is Team O's turn; show another Word Card, and call on a student from Team O to read it.

Variations:

- Students must read the word on the Word Card and read the sentence (or line) in the prayer passage that contains the word before placing a mark in a square. (You can facilitate the game by telling the student which line contains the word.)
- Students must read the Hebrew and give the English meaning before placing an X or an O in a square.
- Students must answer questions about the prayer passage(s) in order to place an X or an O in a square.
- After drawing the Tic-Tac-Toe diagram, write the names of the prayer passages in the squares. Ask each student to choose a square and read the name of the prayer correctly in order to place an X or O in the square.

Beat the Clock

Draw the face of a clock on the chalkboard, but do *not* write the numbers. Draw the hands at the position of 12 o'clock. Think of a word that appears in one of the prayer passages (or ask a student to think of one) and draw horizontal lines on the board—one for each letter in the word. The lines should be next to each other. Then call on individual students to guess which letters are contained in the word. When a student guesses a letter correctly, write that letter over the line that corresponds to the place in the word where the letter appears. If the letter appears more than once, write it on multiple lines. If the student guesses a letter that is not in the word, then add an hour to the face of the clock on the chalkboard; first draw the 1, then the 2, the 3, etc. The object of the game is to guess the word before the clock "strikes 12."

Concentration

Place cards with Hebrew words and cards with the English translations in random order in a pocket chart or on the bottom edge of the chalkboard. Number the backs of the Hebrew words with even numbers and the English words with odd numbers. Then turn the cards over so only the numbers are showing. Ask students individually (or in teams) to try to match the Hebrew and English word pairs by calling out two numbers, one even (for the Hebrew) and one odd (for the English). Turn the two cards over. If they match, then the player scores a point and the matched pair of cards is removed. If they do not match, place the cards back in their original position and ask another student, or the other team, to go. The game continues until all sets have been matched and removed. The player or team with more sets of cards wins.

Hebrew Baseball

Divide the class into two teams. On the board, draw a baseball diamond and a scoreboard. Appoint a student to keep score. Determine the number of words that must be read successfully in order for the reader to earn a "single," "double," "triple," and "home run." Then, as students on each team come "to bat," they can individually decide how many bases to try for—in order to get on base they must then read correctly that number of words from a prayer passage assigned by you. If a student reads incorrectly, he or she is "out" and the next team member goes. After three outs, change teams and repeat. Play for as many innings as you like.

Stop!

This reading game may be used for oral reading practice, review of English meanings, or recognition of prefixes, suffixes, and roots. Assign a student to read until a specific word is reached (for example, instruct the class: "Please read until you come to the Hebrew word for 'ruler.'"). Ask the class to call out "Stop!" when the reader reaches the designated word. Then continue with other students. This game may be played individually or in teams.

Hebrew Bingo

Select 16 Hebrew words or phrases. Prepare a Bingo board with 16 squares. In ten of the squares, chosen at random, write Hebrew words or phrases from among the 16 you selected, leaving the other six squares blank. On a separate piece of paper, draw six boxes (the same size as those on the Bingo board) and write in the remaining six Hebrew words or phrases. Call this card the Extra Word card.

Duplicate enough copies of both the Bingo board and the Extra Word card for every student in your class. Then, have your students cut up the six word boxes on the Extra Word card and paste or tape them at random in the empty boxes on the Bingo board. When the Bingo boards are ready, give each student small objects to use as markers. (The markers can be paper clips, pennies, or any other similar item.) To play, you should call out one of the 16 Hebrew words or phrases for the students to find and cover. The first student to cover four squares in a row (horizontally, vertically, or diagonally), and then read the covered words correctly, wins.

> Variation: Instead of reading the 16 Hebrew words and phrases yourself, cut up one set of the words and phrases into individual words and phrases and place them in a container. Go around the class asking students individually to draw a word or phrase from the container and read it to the class in order to select the square to be covered.

Jeopardy

Create categories by (a) selecting Word Cards and (b) designing 3 x 5 Question Cards about prayers, blessings, rituals, values, etc. The first and easiest item in each category is worth 5 points. As point values increase, the Word Cards and Question Cards progress in difficulty. Write the number of points on the back of each card. Place cards in a pocket chart or on a bulletin board, with the backs facing the students. Label each category.

Divide the class into two or more teams. The first player chooses a category and the degree of difficulty, i.e., the number of points. If the player reads the Word Card correctly or answers the Question Card correctly, the team receives the number of points on the back of the card. The card is then removed from play. If the player's response is incorrect, the card remains in the game and is returned to its original position. Teams alternate. The game continues until all cards have been removed. The team with the most points wins the game.

Siddur Squares

This is a game for the whole class. It can be played using the questions from one of the lessons, or as a review of several lessons.

Select nine students to serve as the "siddur squares." (You might place nine chairs in a Tic-Tac-Toe board arrangement.) Divide the remaining students into two teams, X and O. You or a student can serve as moderator.

The first player on Team X will select one of the nine siddur squares, and the moderator will ask one of the prepared questions from the lesson being reviewed. The siddur square student should give an answer, and the Team X player must agree or disagree with the answer. If the Team X player is correct (that is, agrees with a correct answer or disagrees with an incorrect answer), then Team X should receive an X in that square. You may wish to draw a Tic-Tac-Toe board on the chalkboard to facilitate score keeping.

Continue in the same fashion with Team O. Continue, alternating teams, until one team has three squares in a row, diagonally, vertically, or horizontally.

Matching Questions with Answers

Write questions about the prayer passages on colored paper and put them in a box. Write answers to the questions on white paper and put them in a second box. Divide the class into Team A and Team B. Ask each student on Team A to take a question from the question box, and each student on Team B to take an answer from the answer box. Ask a player from Team A to read his or her question, and ask a student from Team B who thinks his or her card has the correct answer to read the card. Continue this way, asking another Team A member to read a question, and Team B to try to find the correct answer. After all the questions and answers have been correctly matched, collect and return them to their respective boxes and reverse the assignments so that members of Team B have the questions, and Team A the answers.

II. USING THE TEXTBOOK

INTRODUCING THE TEXTBOOK

Draw students' attention to the title of the book, "הִנֵּנִי."

Explain:

הִנֵּנִי means "Here I am" (הִנֵּה אֲנִי). The deep significance of the reply, הִנֵּנִי, is apparent from the first time it is used in the Torah. Abraham was the first person to answer הִנֵּנִי when God called upon him. His answer indicated his readiness to serve God (Genesis 22:1–3).

Generations later, God called to Moses from the burning bush. Again, the answer was הִנֵּנִי (Exodus 3:1–4), and Moses served God by leading the Children of Israel out of Egypt.

And yet generations later, Samuel expressed his readiness to serve God as a prophet when he said הִנֵּנִי (I Samuel 3).

The reply הִנֵּנִי indicates a readiness to listen and to serve God through action. You have heard your name and understand it to be a personal call. When we say הִנֵּנִי today, we indicate a willingness to step forward and continue in the tradition of our ancestors. With our faith in God, with God's faith in our abilities, and with assistance from others, we are ready to accomplish all that is before us.

LESSON 1
אֵין כָּמוֹךָ\אַב הָרַחֲמִים

LEARNING OBJECTIVES

Prayer Reading Skills
- The prefixes בְּ ("among the" or "in the"); וְ ("and")
- The suffix ךָ ("you" or "your")
- The roots מלכ ("rule"); עשׂה ("do" or "make"); רחמ ("mercy" or "compassion")
- The words כְּמוֹ ("like"); כָּמוֹךָ = כְּמוֹ + ךָ ("like you")
- God's name is written יְיָ, יְהֹוָה (Adonai)

Prayer Concepts
God:
- God is, was, and always will be.
- God is merciful and compassionate.
- We call God אַב הָרַחֲמִים ("merciful parent").
- We place our trust in God.

Torah:
- We thank God for the Torah.
- The Torah symbolizes our connection to our ancestors and descendants, and to God.

The Torah Service:
- The Torah service begins with a reference to God, not to the Torah.
- The Torah service has three main parts: taking the Torah from the Ark, reading the Torah, returning the Torah to the Ark.

BEYOND THE TEXTBOOK
- The double *sh'va*
- The *dagesh* that does not change the sound of a letter
- The final ךָ

ABOUT THE PRAYER
The Torah service begins with prayers praising God, not the Torah itself. Reading the Torah is central to the synagogue service.

INSTRUCTIONAL MATERIALS

Text pages 4–13

Word Cards 1–11

Worksheet 1

Family Education: "As a Family: The Beginning" (at the back of this guide)

SET INDUCTION

Introduce the Torah service with a class visit to the sanctuary. (Be sure to get permission first.) Have students gather around the *Aron Hakodesh*, the Holy Ark. Talk about the design of the Ark as well as the design and placement of the *ner tamid*, the Eternal Light above the Ark that symbolizes God's eternal presence.

Open the Ark and examine the garments and ornaments that adorn the *sefer Torah*, the Torah scroll. These ritual items set the tone for the Torah service and the rituals that follow. Many of the items represent the clothing worn by the High Priest (Exodus 39:1–31).

Point out the following to the students:

- the *keter Torah*, silver crown of the Torah, or the *rimonim*, silver ornaments found atop the wooden rollers of the Torah scroll
- the *m'il*, mantle, which covers and protects the Torah scroll
- the *hoshen*, breastplate, placed over the mantle
- the *hagorah*, belt, which wraps around the Torah and holds the scroll in place
- the *yad*, "hand" or pointer, used to point to the words in the Torah during the reading

A Blessing

Teach the students the blessing we say when we study Torah.

בָּרוּךְ אַתָּה, יְיָ אֱלֹהֵינוּ, מֶלֶךְ הָעוֹלָם,
אֲשֶׁר קִדְּשָׁנוּ בְּמִצְוֹתָיו וְצִוָּנוּ
לַעֲסוֹק בְּדִבְרֵי תוֹרָה.

Praised are You, Adonai our God, Ruler of the universe, who has made us holy through mitzvot and commands us to engage in the study of Torah.

INTO THE TEXT

Call on students to read aloud the first paragraph introducing the lesson.

Ask students how we can show our appreciation for a gift. (*by saying thank you, writing a note, calling, using the gift*)

Have students read the second paragraph of the introduction aloud.

As a Family

You may wish to send home a copy of "As a Family: The Beginning," with each student, at this time.

Into the Prayer

- Call on students to read the Hebrew prayer aloud.
- Write the word וּמֶמְשַׁלְתְּךָ (line 2) on the chalkboard as follows: וּ מֶמְ שַׁל תְּךָ.
- Call on students to read each word-part and then the whole word. Point out that when there is a double *sh'va* (לְתְּ), the first *sh'va* is silent and the letter over it is blended with the letter-vowel combination that precedes it (שַׁל). The second *sh'va* is sounded (תְּךָ).
- Call on students to read each word that has a final ךָ.
- Ask students to read the word(s):
  built on the root מלכ, "rule." (מַלְכוּתְךָ, מַלְכוּת, מֶלֶךְ, יִמְלֹךְ)
  built on the root ברכ, "bless." (יְבָרֵךְ)
  meaning "with peace." (בְשָׁלוֹם)

PRAYER DICTIONARY

Note: The English meaning is on the back of each Word Card.

Display Word Cards 2–5.

Call on students to read each word and its English meaning. Ask:

- What suffix appears on Word Cards 2–5 (ךָ) and what does it mean? (*"you" or "yours," singular*)

- Distribute Word Cards 2–5 to four students. Call on the four students in turn to read their assigned Word Card, but have them stop before the final ךָ. The class should read the suffix in unison. (For example, Word Card 2: *Student*—כְּמוֹ; *Class*—ךָ.)

- Repeat the activity with four different students until everyone has a turn.

ALL YOURS

Have students complete the activity using the Prayer Dictionary to assist them.

Check their answers or have them check each other's answers.

Photo Op

Note: "Photo Op" offers the teacher and students the opportunity to broaden class discussions using photographs that appear throughout the text.

Direct the students to the photograph in the middle of page 5. Read the caption aloud.

Ask: What makes a gift precious? (*the giver and the receiver have a special relationship; it's something the receiver has always wanted; the gift is made or chosen with love and care; it's rare*)

PAST, PRESENT, FUTURE

Display Word Cards 6–8.

Call on students to read each word in unison. Repeat, each time displaying the words at a faster pace for fun and fluency. Review the English meaning of each word.

Have students complete the activity independently and then review as a class.

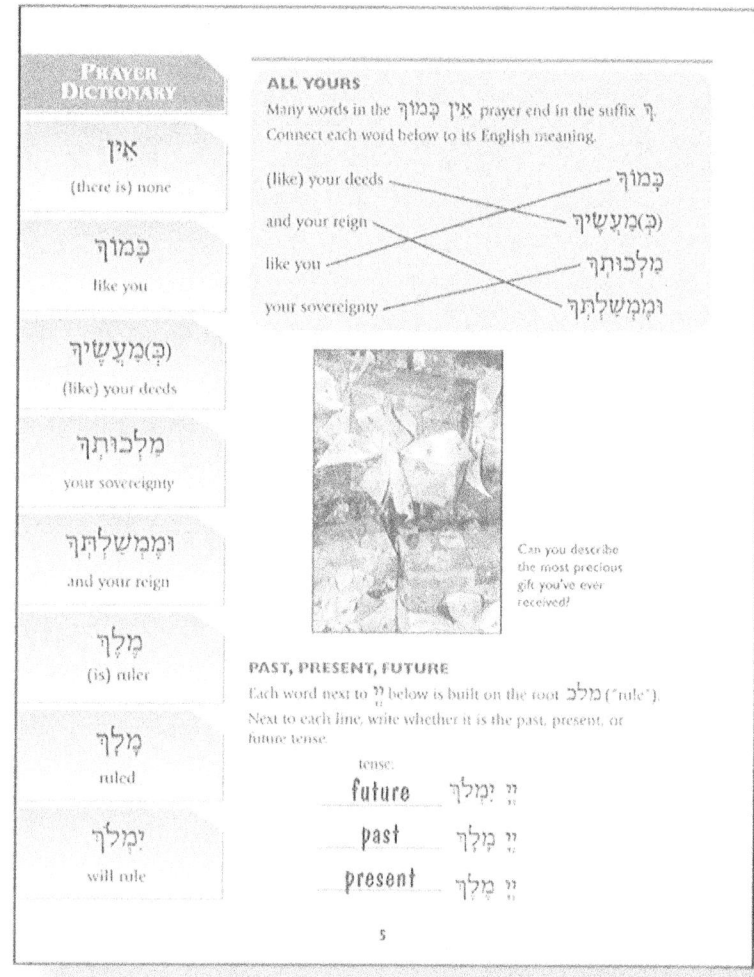

The Fruit of the Tree

Start "planting an orchard" in your classroom.

Create a "tree" with three roots from oaktag, poster board, or construction paper. On each of the roots of the tree, write one letter: מלכ. Write the word "rule" on the trunk.

Let students choose the kind of fruit they would like to grow on their מלכ tree and cut out the shapes of the fruit. (*orange tree—orange paper; banana tree—yellow paper; apple tree—red or green paper*)

On each "fruit," write a different Hebrew word that "grows" from the root מלכ.

Begin with the Prayer Dictionary words on page 5. (מַלְכוּתְךָ, מֶלֶךְ, מָלַךְ, יִמְלֹךְ)

Challenge students to find, read, and add another word built on the root מלכ from page 4, line 1. (מַלְכוּת) Each time students learn new words built on this root, add them to the tree. Each time a new root is introduced in the text, add a new fruit tree to the orchard. **Note:** Make the fruits removable to play reading games.

> **TORAH SERVICE**
>
> What do you like about going to the movies with your friends? Maybe it's the popcorn. Or maybe it's getting seats together and talking until the lights go out. Or maybe you can't wait to see the coming attractions. But the part we all look forward to the most—the highlight of our experience—is seeing the movie itself! In the same way, the Torah service is the highlight of all the prayers in our synagogue service, many of which come from the Torah (for example, מִי כָמֹכָה, שְׁמַע, and וְאָהַבְתָּ).
>
> The Torah is the first part of the Hebrew Bible. In it we read the stories of our ancestors. But the Torah is far more than a textbook like the one you study in history class. Not only does it tell the story of our ancestors, it also symbolizes our connection to them and to God. In the thousands of years since we received the Torah, the Jewish people have been reading it over and over again, passing down its teachings from generation to generation.
>
> Most congregations read a portion of the Torah on Shabbat morning and on certain Jewish holidays. Others read from the Torah on Friday evenings. In some congregations, a portion of the Torah is read on Mondays and Thursdays, too. The Torah service itself has three main parts: taking the Torah out of the Ark, reading the Torah, and returning the Torah to the Ark. Each part of the Torah service has its own blessings and ceremonies.
>
>
>
> Parents and children can work together to better understand the teachings of our tradition.
>
> 6

TORAH SERVICE

The Five Books of Moses

Write the English and Hebrew names of the books of the *Humash* on the chalkboard in right-to-left order.

בְּרֵאשִׁית	שְׁמוֹת	וַיִּקְרָא	בְּמִדְבַּר	דְּבָרִים
Genesis	Exodus	Leviticus	Numbers	Deuteronomy

(displayed right-to-left: Deuteronomy Numbers Leviticus Exodus Genesis)

Call on students to chant the English names of the books in order.

Then ask them to chant the Hebrew names. Challenge individual students to recite all five Hebrew names by heart.

Call out the Hebrew name of a book. Have the students respond by saying the matching English name. Repeat the activity by giving the English name.

Have individual students read page 6 aloud.

Ask: Why is the Torah service the highlight of the synagogue service? (*the Torah is the source of the mitzvot; the Torah tells the story of our ancestors; it symbolizes our connection to previous generations and to God; it is part of our heritage*)

Call on students to write the three main parts of the Torah service on the chalkboard.

Photo Op

Direct the students to the photograph on page 6. Read the caption aloud.

Jewish tradition teaches that adults are responsible for passing the teachings of the Torah on to the next generation, the children. How can adults fulfill this obligation? (*send children to religious school; study at home together; read and discuss the Torah portion of the week; celebrate Jewish holidays and life-cycle events together*)

PRAYER BUILDING BLOCKS

The Prayer Building Blocks feature recurs throughout the text. It highlights specific words and phrases from the lesson's prayer. It often focuses on roots, prefixes, and suffixes to help students understand the meaning of prayer words.

אֵין כָּמוֹךָ בָאֱלֹהִים
"there is none like you among the gods (other people worship)"

Read the Building Block with the students.

Part 1: כְּמוֹ + ךָ = כָּמוֹךָ

Ask students for English contractions.
(*do + not=don't*)

Part 2: אֱלֹהִים ("gods")

Explain that the word אֱלֹהִים is one of many Hebrew names for God. It can also mean "gods."

Call on a student to read the paragraph in the middle of page 7 ("The word 'gods' has…").

Part 3: Chant the Sh'ma with the students. Allow a few minutes for students to write the English meaning of the Sh'ma in the text.

DID YOU NOTICE?

Read the statement and question aloud.

Form *hevruta* discussion groups of two or three students each. Allow each *hevruta* time to discuss possible responses to the question. Direct the students to write their responses on the lines provided. Call on the groups to share their responses.

Note: The term *hevruta* is built on the Hebrew word *haver* ("friend" or "colleague").

אֵין כָּמוֹךָ בָאֱלֹהִים "there is none like you among the gods (other people worship)"

אֵין means "(there is) none."
כָּמוֹךָ is made up of two parts:
כְּמוֹ means "like."
ךָ is a suffix meaning "you" or "your."

Sometimes, when you add a suffix to a word, it changes the word's letters or vowels (כְּמוֹ + ךָ = כָּמוֹךָ).

בָאֱלֹהִים means "among the gods."
בָּ is a prefix meaning "among the" or "in the."
אֱלֹהִים means "gods."

The word "gods" has a small "g" because it refers to pagan gods that people worshipped in ancient times. We write the name of our God with a capital "G" because there is only One God.

The Sh'ma expresses this belief:

שְׁמַע יִשְׂרָאֵל: יְיָ אֱלֹהֵינוּ, יְיָ אֶחָד.

Write the English meaning of the Sh'ma below.

Hear O Israel: Adonai is our God, Adonai is One.

 DID YOU NOTICE?
The Torah service begins with a reference to God, not to the Torah itself. Why do you think the Torah service praises God first?

The Torah was given to us by God.
We acknowledge God before all else.

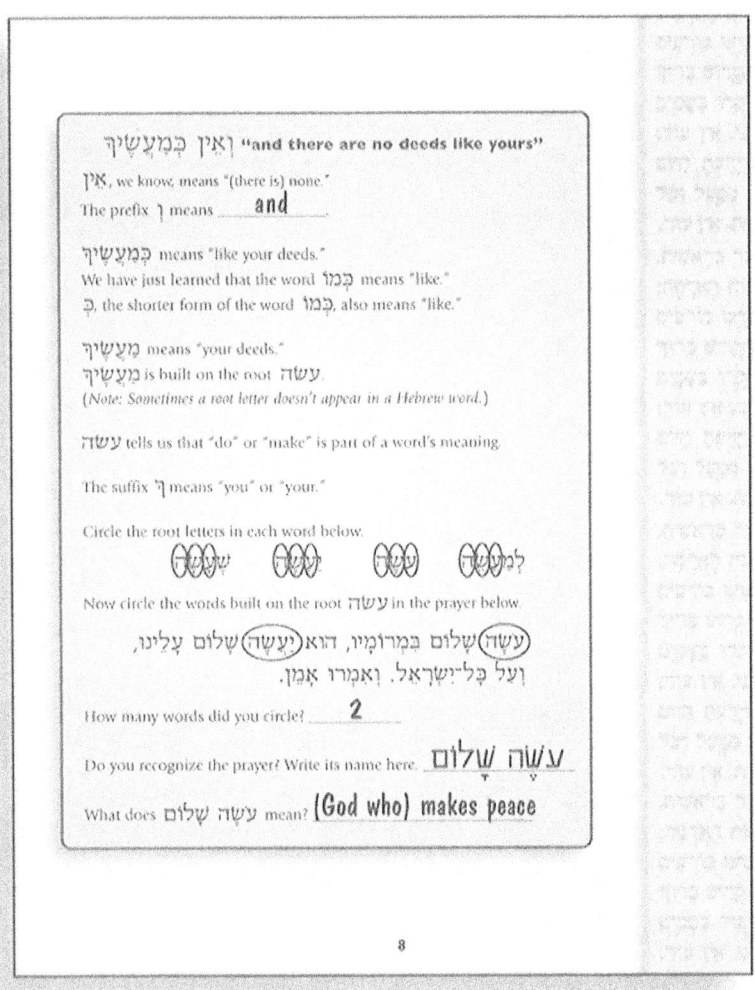

The Fruit of the Tree

Create a fruit tree with the root עשׂה. Write "do" and "make" on the trunk. Write כְּמַעֲשֶׂיךָ on a fruit for the tree.

Add fruit to the tree using words built on the root עשׂה.

Write the name of the prayer, עֹשֶׂה שָׁלוֹם, on a fruit and add it to the tree.

וְאֵין כְּמַעֲשֶׂיךָ
"and there are no deeds like yours"

Read the Building Block with the students.

כְּמַעֲשֶׂיךָ means "like your deeds."

Direct students to page 4, lines 1–2, in their texts.

Read the first sentence in unison with students. (אֵין...כְּמַעֲשֶׂיךָ)

Then read the second sentence in unison with students. (מַלְכוּתְךָ...דּוֹר וָדֹר)

A Partnership

Have students count off 1–2, 1–2, around the room to form reading partnerships.

Have Partner 1 read page 4, sentence 1. Partner 2 reads sentence 2. Then have partners reverse roles.

Teach students to sing the two sentences using your synagogue's melody.

Review the English meaning of these sentences. (*There is…generation to generation*)

A New Root

Direct students back to page 8.

Continue in the middle of the page: מַעֲשֶׂיךָ means "your deeds."

Read the four words built on the root עשׂה.

Read the prayer that concludes the Building Block, Oseh Shalom.

Teach the students to sing the prayer using your synagogue's melody.

יְיָ מֶלֶךְ, יְיָ מָלָךְ, יְיָ יִמְלֹךְ לְעוֹלָם וָעֶד

"Adonai is ruler, Adonai ruled, Adonai will rule forever and ever"

Read the Building Block with the students.

Call on students to read aloud each circled word in the activity. (See page 14 of this Teacher's Edition.)
(מַלְכוּתְךָ, מַלְכוּת, מֶלֶךְ, מָלָךְ, יִמְלֹךְ)

A Partnership

Have students pair off in the same reading partnerships they formed previously.

Have the partners read lines 3 and 4 on page 4, the same way they did before.

Teach students to sing the lines using your synagogue's melody.

Review the English meaning of these sentences. (*Adonai is Ruler...with peace*)

Call on the students to read and then sing page 4, lines 1–4.

FROM THE SOURCES

Call on students to read each biblical verse aloud.

Direct their attention to the citations.

Ask: Which selection is from the Torah? (*Exodus 15:18*)

In which section of the Bible do we find Psalms? (*the third section: Writings*—כְּתוּבִים)

Reading Citations

Write the citations on the chalkboard: Psalm 10:16; Psalm 96:10; Exodus 15:18.

Explain that the first number is the chapter number. The second number is the verse number. Call on individual students to name each citation in the following way: Book of Psalms, Chapter 10, Verse 16, and so on for each one.

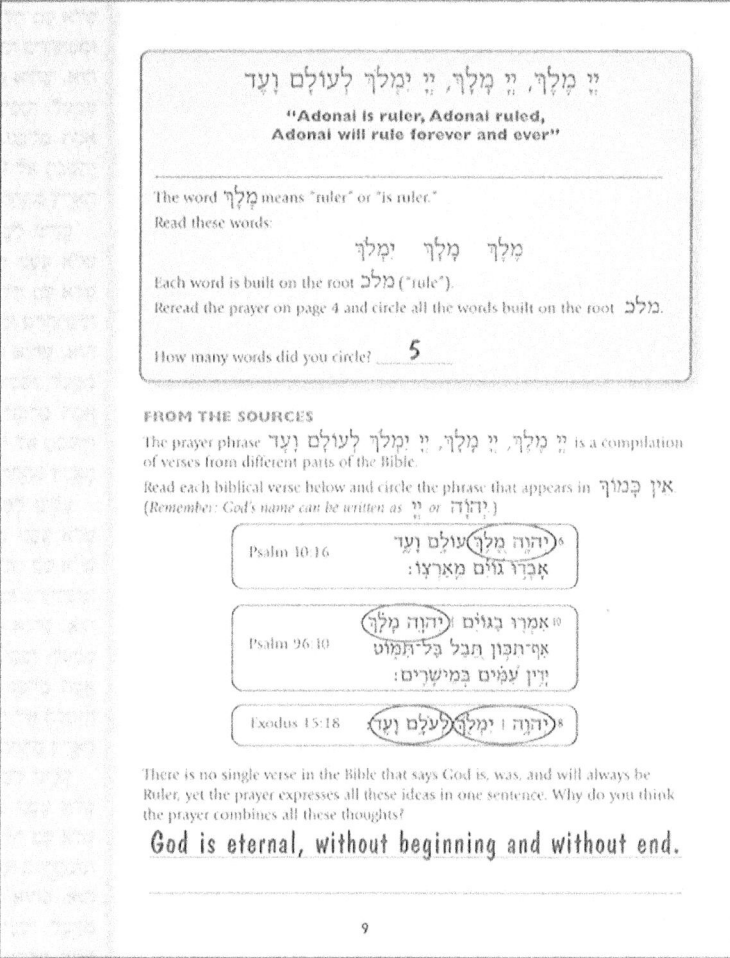

Ḥevruta

Have students form study groups to respond to the question at the bottom of the page. Call on the groups to share their responses.

INTRODUCING אַב הָרַחֲמִים

Have students read aloud the introduction on page 10.

Ask them for examples of people they trust in their own lives.

Into the Prayer

Reading Rule: The *dagesh* is the dot in the middle of a letter. Sometimes the dot changes the sound of a letter (בּב, כּכ, פּפ); sometimes it does not (מ, נ, ל).

Call on students to read each word in the prayer with a *dagesh* that does *not* change the sound of the letter. (צִיּוֹן, תִּבְנֶה, וְנִשָּׂא)

Then have them read the phrases in which those words appear.

Reading Practice

Choose two students. The first student should read the English meaning of the prayer aloud, pausing at each comma, semicolon, and period.

The second student should read each corresponding Hebrew phrase. (example: "merciful parent"—אַב הָרַחֲמִים)

Repeat the activity with different pairs of students.

Call on individual students to read the complete prayer.

PRAYER DICTIONARY

Display Word Cards 9–11. Call on students to read each word aloud. Review the English meaning of each.

WHAT'S MISSING?

Direct students to complete the phrases by choosing the correct Word Card. Have students cover the Prayer Dictionary while working on the exercise. They can then uncover it and check their own answers.

Photo Op

Direct students to the photograph in the middle of the page. Read the caption aloud.

Ask students to share occasions when they put their trust in someone and the person proved to be trustworthy. Now ask them to share times when they themselves proved to be trustworthy. Try to limit the discussion to positive examples.

MERCIFUL PARENT

Read this section aloud with the students.

Ask: What does it mean to be "compassionate"? Have a dictionary handy so students can look up the meaning of the word. (*sympathetic; showing concern*)

Explain that there are many Hebrew names for God. Each name symbolizes a different aspect of our relationship with God. Children, too, sometimes refer to their parents with different terms in different contexts.

The Fruit of the Tree

Create a fruit tree with the roots רחמ.

Write "mercy" and "compassion" on the trunk.

Create three fruits, one for each name for God built on the root רחמ, and add it to the tree.

21 LESSON 1

FROM THE SOURCES

Read the first paragraph aloud.

Note: Zion, צִיּוֹן, is also used to refer to all of Israel—אֶרֶץ צִיּוֹן.

Have students read the selection from Psalm 51 and follow the directions.

Chapter and Verse

Ask: Which two verses from Psalm 51 did you read? (*verses 19 and 20*)

Which verse is included in אַב הָרַחֲמִים? (*verse 20*)

Call on students to read Psalm 51, Verse 20 aloud.

Vocabulary Review

Ask students which words in Psalm 51, Verse 20 mean:

- Zion. (צִיּוֹן)
- Jerusalem. (יְרוּשָׁלָיִם)

What is the English meaning of verse 20?
Hint: Students should look on page 10 in their texts. (*favor Zion with Your goodness; rebuild the walls of Jerusalem*)

WHOM DO YOU TRUST?

Read the activity aloud.

Allow students time to consider their responses. Review their answers together.

FLUENT READING

Display an Israeli flag in class.

Talk about the design of the flag. The two blue stripes represent the blue stripes of a *tallit*. The Jewish Star, *Magen David* ("Shield of David"), is a symbol of the Jewish people. Some say King David had this star on his shield when he went into battle.

Read the introduction on page 13 aloud.

Explain that *Hatikvah* means "The Hope."

Have students draw a *Magen David* above the word הַתִּקְוָה each time a form of the word appears in the anthem. ("our hope"—תִּקְוָתֵנוּ; "the hope"—הַתִּקְוָה)

Read the English translation of the anthem. Ask:

- What hope is expressed in the anthem? (*that we return to our land as a free people*)
- Do you think this hope has been fulfilled? (*yes: we have a Jewish state in Israel; no: the Jewish people are still not at peace in the land, not free to live without fear*)

Read *Hatikvah* in unison with the students.

Call on individual students to take turns reading.

Stand and face the Israeli flag. Teach the students to sing *Hatikvah*.

Art Project

Have students make an Israeli flag using blue and white art materials (crayons, paints, tissue paper, felt). Duplicate *Hatikvah* and have them paste it on the back of their flags.

WORKSHEET

Duplicate and hand out copies of the worksheet for Lesson 1 to review skills and concepts.

FAMILY EDUCATION

Duplicate and send home copies of "As a Family: The Beginning" (at the back of this guide) if you did not already do so.

LESSON 1
Worksheet

Name: _____

אֵין כָּמוֹךָ \ אַב הָרַחֲמִים

1. Complete the prayer sentence below by filling in the Hebrew words in the order in which they appear in the prayer. יִמְלֹךְ   מֶלֶךְ   מָלָךְ

   יְיָ _____, יְיָ _____, יְיָ _____ לְעוֹלָם וָעֶד.

   Adonai is <u>Ruler</u>, Adonai <u>ruled</u>, Adonai will <u>rule</u> forever and ever.

   What is the root of the three Hebrew words you wrote? ____ ____ ____

2. Write the root of each Hebrew word on the first line below it. (*Note: Sometimes a root letter doesn't appear in a word.*) Then write the English equivalent of the root on the second line.

   עָשָׂה   מַלְכוּתְךָ   רַחוּם   כְּמַעֲשֶׂיךָ   הָרַחֲמִים   מַלְכוּת

   _____ _____ _____ _____ _____ _____

   _____ _____ _____ _____ _____ _____

3. Add the suffix ךָ to complete each word.

   כְּמוֹ___   קָדְשׁ___   וּמֶמְשַׁלְתְּ___   שִׁמְ___

   What does the suffix ךָ mean? _____

4. Read the following line from אַב הָרַחֲמִים, then answer the questions that follow.

   אַב הָרַחֲמִים, הֵיטִיבָה בִרְצוֹנְךָ אֶת־צִיּוֹן; תִּבְנֶה חוֹמוֹת יְרוּשָׁלָיִם.

   Which Hebrew word means "father" or "parent"? _____

   Write the word for "Jerusalem." _____

   Which word is another name for Jerusalem? _____

5. The Torah service has three main parts. Fill in the missing parts on the blank lines below.

   1. _____
   2. _____
   3. Returning the Torah to the Ark

LESSON 2
כִּי מִצִּיּוֹן לְךָ יְיָ

LEARNING OBJECTIVES

Prayer Reading Skills

- The prefixes מִ ("from"); וּ ("and"); שֶׁ ("who"); לְ ("to"); בְּ ("in")
- The word ending וֹ ("his")
- The roots דבר ("speak," "word," or "thing"); קדש ("holy")
- Zion, צִיּוֹן, is another name for Jerusalem, יְרוּשָׁלַיִם
- Torah means "teaching" or "instruction"

Prayer Concepts

- The teachings of the Torah are passed down from one generation to the next.
- We pray that Torah and Israel will be our sources of strength throughout the generations.
- We honor and respect the Torah, but we worship God.
- The Torah scroll is carried among the congregants in anticipation of the Torah reading.
- Congregants traditionally show respect and love for the Torah by touching it with their *tallit* or *siddur*, which they then bring to their lips.
- Traditionally, we read from the Torah on Shabbat, on holidays, and on Mondays and Thursdays.

BEYOND THE TEXTBOOK

Reading Rules:

- The letter *vav* with a *dagesh*, the dot in the middle of a letter (וּ)
- The ending vowel sounds "eye" (אַי) and "ahv" (אָיו)
- Double letters with the sounded *sh'va* (מְמַ)

The word נְבִיאִים ("prophets")

ABOUT THE PRAYER

When we open the Ark for the Torah service, we recall the first Ark that the people of Israel carried through the desert in Moses' time (Numbers 10:33–36). The teachings of the Torah have since been passed down through the generations. The opening verses of the Torah service link us to the land of Israel and to Jerusalem, the site of the First and Second Temples. As the *sefer Torah* is carried to the reader's table, we each have the opportunity to be close to the Torah and to reach out to it.

INSTRUCTIONAL MATERIALS

Text pages 14–23

Word Cards 12–18

Worksheet 2

Family Education: "As a Family: From Generation to Generation" (at the back of this guide)

SET INDUCTION

For Discussion

What is a ritual? (*a prescribed order of ceremonies or actions; a gesture or activity that has symbolic importance, for example, lighting Shabbat candles*)

Why is the order of the rituals important? (*we know what to expect; each step in the order prepares us for the next step*)

Discuss the difference between a routine and a ritual. (*routines have no specific embedded meanings; examples of routines: switch off alarm in morning, brush teeth, eat breakfast, do homework in afternoon*)

Jewish Rituals

Discuss the rituals we follow when we welcome Shabbat. List them in order on the chalkboard. (<u>to prepare for Shabbat</u>: *buy or bake hallah, prepare the meal, set out Shabbat candles, wine, hallah;* <u>to welcome Shabbat</u>: *sing Shalom Aleichem, recite the blessings*)

Talk about the rituals that comprise the Passover seder. (<u>to prepare for Passover</u>: *remove hametz; set the Passover table with ritual items such as candlesticks, wine, matzah, seder plate;* <u>during the seder</u>: *read from the haggadah; follow the steps of the seder*)

The Torah Service

The rituals for the Torah service honor God and connect us to previous generations; for example, opening the Ark reminds us of the first Ark the Jews carried in the desert on the journey to the Promised Land (Exodus 25:10–16). Some rituals reflect honor and respect for the Torah, for example, dressing the Torah in decorative covers and housing it in a beautiful and protective Ark, reciting special prayers, and carrying it among the congregants.

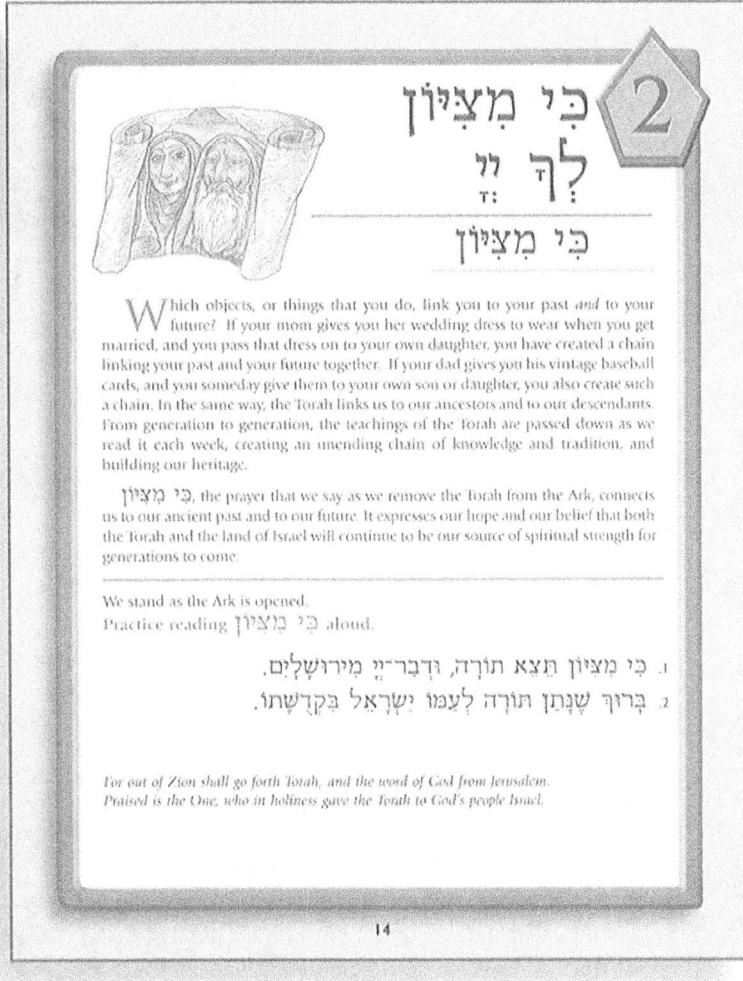

Reading Practice

Have students read the prayer in Hebrew.

Call on half the class to read line 1 and half to read line 2.

Reverse reading roles.

INTO THE TEXT
Visualizing the Ritual

Create three headings for a bulletin board or wall display for each of the parts of the Torah service: taking the Torah from the Ark, reading the Torah, returning the Torah to the Ark. Consider mounting each heading inside a Torah scroll design.

As the students learn prayers and discuss rituals, list them under the appropriate heading. When holding a model service, take photos and add them to the display.

Begin by reviewing the prayers in Lesson 1, pages 4 and 10. (אֵין כָּמוֹךָ, אַב הָרַחֲמִים)

Write the name of each prayer under the heading "Taking the Torah from the Ark."

Call on a student to read aloud the English introduction to the lesson on page 14. Ask: What heirlooms, objects, or traditions have been passed down in your family?

Add the name of the prayer, כִּי מִצִּיּוֹן, to the bulletin board display under the heading "Taking the Torah from the Ark."

As a Family

You might wish to duplicate and send home the "As a Family: From Generation to Generation" page at this time.

Into the Prayer

Ask students to read aloud the English meaning of the prayer.

Explain that "Zion" is the name of one of the hills in Jerusalem. Zion can also refer to all of Jerusalem and all of Israel. "Zionism" is a movement calling on Jews to settle in Israel and supporting the right of Israel to exist.

Show students a map of Israel. Locate Jerusalem on the map.

PRAYER DICTIONARY

Display Word Cards 12, 13, and 15. Call on students to read each word.

Ask students to explain the relationship between the words. (*"from Zion" and "from Jerusalem" refer to the same place since "Zion" can also mean all of Israel; the prayer says that "Torah" or "teaching" emanates from Zion*)

Vocabulary Challenge

Hold up Word Cards 12–18 one at a time in random order. Ask the students to find the English meaning in the Prayer Dictionary. Tell them to prepare for a vocabulary challenge. Have students close their texts and form two teams.

Again, display Word Cards 12–18 one at a time in random order. This time, ask students to give the English meaning of each word from memory. Allow team members to confer about their answers.

MATCH GAME

Have students cover the Prayer Dictionary and complete the exercise, then uncover it to check their own answers.

Photo Op

Read the caption aloud to students. Discuss the meaning of the word "nurture." (*give nourishment; train; support*) Ask: How can parents instill in their children the ability to love and nurture? (*by giving the child respect and affection; by acting as a role model; by supporting the child's dreams and goals; by helping others*)

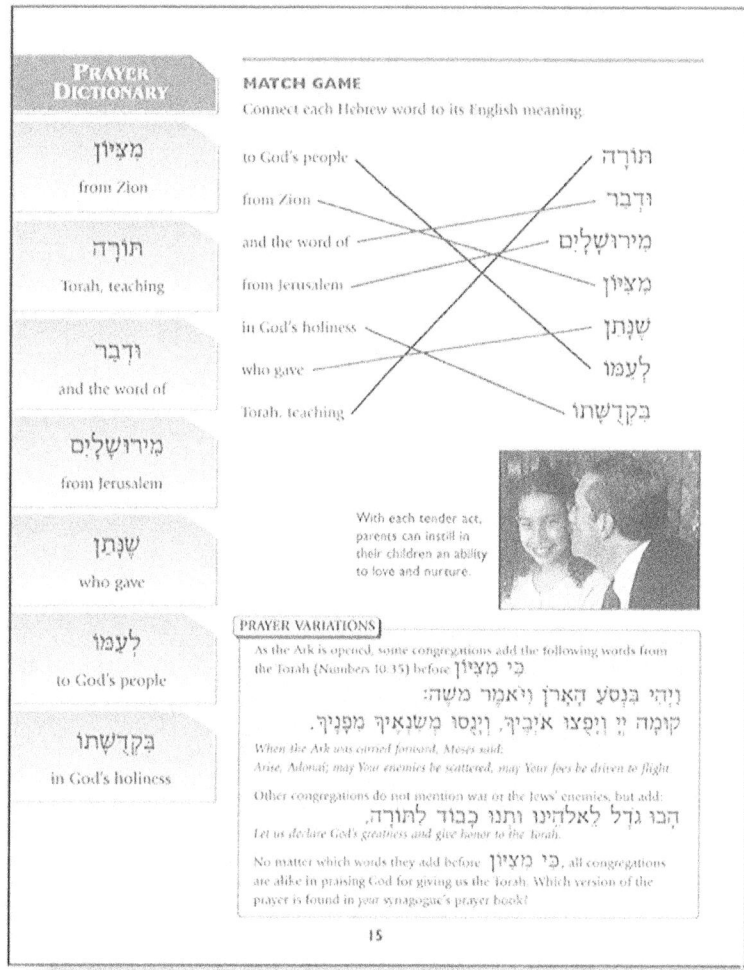

PRAYER VARIATIONS

Read this section aloud with students. Call on individual students to read the Hebrew selections.

Have students find the Torah service in your synagogue's prayerbook to answer the question at the bottom of the page.

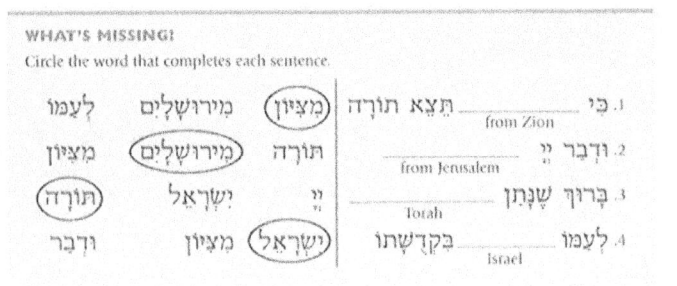

WHAT'S MISSING?

Have students complete the exercise.

Call on students to read each completed phrase, 1–4.

Ask students for the meaning of the two words *not* circled on each line.

OUT OF ORDER

Challenge students to complete each section from memory. Students can check their answers on page 14 in the text.

Have a student read the first set of words in the correct order. Have another student read the second set of words in the correct order.

Reinforcing Word Order

Choose one of the techniques in Reinforcing Word Order at the front of this guide.

Photo Op

Read the caption to students. The Old City is a walled city within Jerusalem. There are eight gates in the wall that surrounds the Old City. King David's Tower, also known as the Citadel (fortress), is next to the Jaffa Gate. The tower is associated with King David—who conquered Jerusalem and made it the religious and political center of Israel—because it is so imposing.

TORAH READING

On separate, numbered index cards, write key words and phrases in the order in which they appear in this section. Give each student an index card.

Direct the students to find and underline their word or phrase in the text, and have them prepare to explain its meaning to the class. Sample words and phrases include: Monday and Thursday, Ezra the scribe, Babylonia, Rosh Hashanah, Sukkot, 586 BCE.

Call on students to explain their key word or phrase *in numbered order* so that together you answer the question, "How did the custom of reading the Torah originate?" Then have the students fill in the answer to the first question on the page.

Sharing

Direct students to the second question on the page.

Form *hevruta* discussion groups of three students each to discuss the question. Have each member record the group's responses on the lines provided. Ask the groups to share their insights with the entire class.

Extending the Ritual

Read a selection from Torah (the *humash*) each week in class.

Suggested selections:

- a passage from *parashat hashavua*, the Torah portion of the week
- the description of the building of the Tabernacle in the desert (Exodus 35)
- the description of the High Priest's dress, today reflected in the way we dress the Torah (Exodus 28)
- a passage that reflects an upcoming holiday
- a reference to Shabbat (e.g., Genesis 2:1–3, Exodus 20:8–11, Exodus 31:16–17)

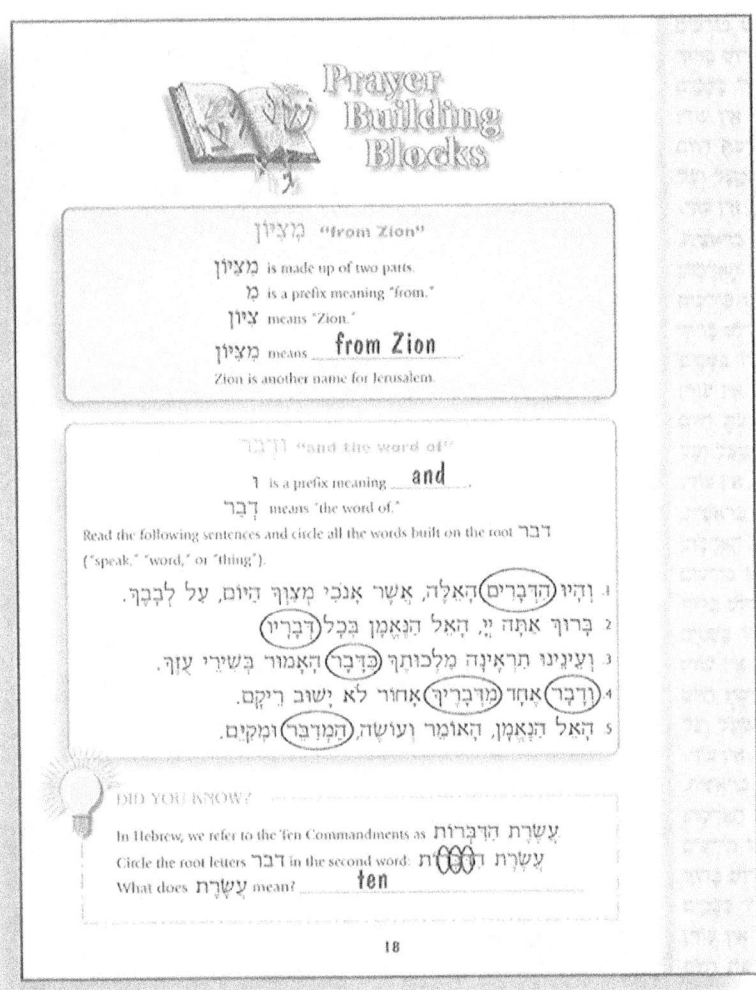

The Fruit of the Tree

Create a fruit tree with the root דבר. Write "speak," "word," and "thing" on the trunk.

Write the word וּדְבַר and all the circled words on page 18 on fruit for the tree. Create a fruit for the phrase עֲשֶׂרֶת הַדִּבְּרוֹת (Ten Commandments).

PRAYER BUILDING BLOCKS

מִצִּיּוֹן "from Zion"

Read and complete the Building Block together.

Review with students the meaning of the term "Zionism." (*a movement supporting the right of the Jewish state of Israel to exist, founded by Theodor Herzl in 1897; a philosophy that Jews have an obligation to make aliyah*)

וּדְבַר "and the word of"

Call on students to circle each word built on the root דבר.

Reading Rule

When the letter ו contains a *dagesh*—a dot in the middle (וּ), it looks like the vowel "oo" (וּ).

ו is a letter, and not a vowel, if

- the letter before it already has a vowel. (צַו)
- the ו has its own vowel. (וֹ)

Call on students to read the word in line 1 that has a *vav* with a *dagesh*. (מִצֻוָּךְ)

Reading Rule

When ָ is followed by a *yud* (י), together they have the sound "eye." (אַי)

When a ו follows "eye" at the end of a word, we pronounce the ending "ahv." (אָיו)

Call on students to read the word in line 2 that has the ending sound "ahv." (דְּבָרָיו)

Call on students to read the circled words in lines 1–5 and then to read each complete line.

מִירוּשָׁלַיִם "from Jerusalem"

Read the Building Block with the students.

Write the word נְבִיאִים on the chalkboard. Explain that נְבִיאִים means "prophets." In ancient times the prophets were people who spoke on behalf of God. The teachings of the prophets comprise the second section of the Bible.

Note: Lesson 4 covers the three sections of the Bible.

Call on students to read Isaiah's words, "For out of Zion shall go forth Torah, and the word of God from Jerusalem," in Hebrew.

Discuss the meaning of the quotation from Isaiah: "they shall beat their swords...nation against nation..." (*the world will be at peace; people will work with each other instead of against each other*)

Play the following game to practice lines 1–5.

Strike 12!

Draw a clock on the chalkboard and write the number 12 in the 12 o'clock position. In place of the other numbers, write a selection of any Hebrew letters from lines 1–5. Ask a player to select a letter on the clock and read one word from lines 1–5 containing that letter, naming the position on the clock. For example: The player might select the letter נ located at the 8 o'clock position. The player says, "I choose *nun* at 8 o'clock. I will read the fourth word in line 2." If the word is read correctly, the player should replace the letter נ with the number 8 on the clock. A second player then selects another letter in a different position on the clock and the game continues. The game is over when all the letters have been replaced by numbers and the clock strikes 12!

Variation: For a more challenging game, the player should read the word *and* the complete line in which the word is found.

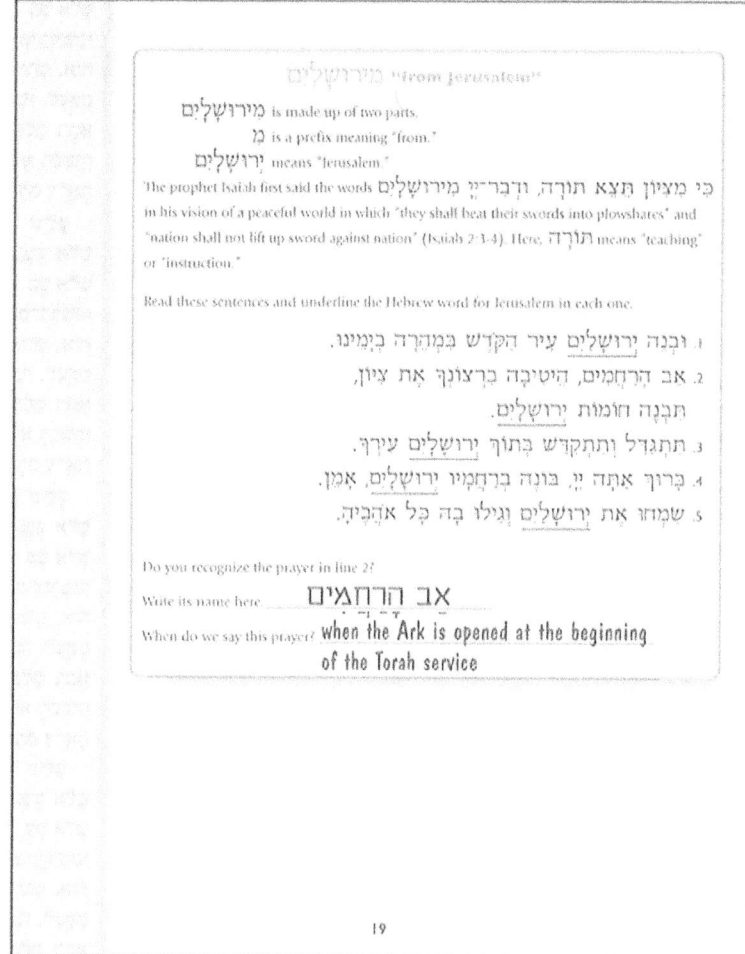

Games...Games...Games

Use the "Classroom Games" section at the front of this guide. Select one or more games to reinforce reading and concepts as students work on the exercises and activities throughout the text.

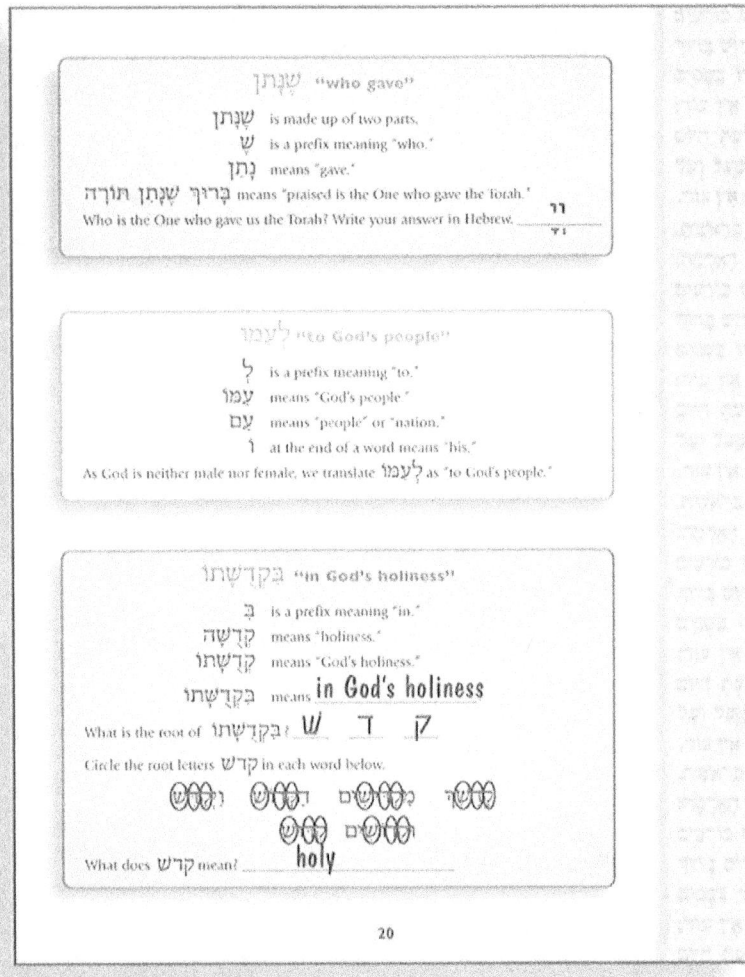

שֶׁנָּתַן "who gave"

Complete the section together.

Think About It

One way we can praise God is with our words.

Discuss ways we can praise God by our actions. (*by fulfilling mitzvot; by acting in God-like ways, such as by showing kindness to others or by protecting and preserving the environment*)

לְעַמּוֹ "to God's people"

Complete the section together.

Introduce the phrase עַם יִשְׂרָאֵל to the students. Teach them to sing the well-known song that begins: עַם יִשְׂרָאֵל חַי, *The people of Israel live!*

בִּקְדֻשָּׁתוֹ "in God's holiness"

Complete the Building Block with the students.

Direct the students to the six words built on the root קדשׁ.

Ask them to read:

- the three words ending with a final letter. (קָדְשְׁךָ, מַקְדִּישִׁים, וּקְדוֹשִׁים)

- the four words with a *dagesh* that does not change the sound of the letter in which it is found. (מַקְדִּישִׁים, הַקָּדוֹשׁ, וִיקַדֵּשׁ, קִדֵּשׁ)

- the word with the prefix meaning "the." (הַקָּדוֹשׁ)

- the two words with the prefix meaning "and." (וִיקַדֵּשׁ, וּקְדוֹשִׁים)

Ask: Which word is the name of the prayer we chant over wine? (קִדּוּשׁ)

The Fruit of the Tree

Create a fruit tree with the root קדשׁ. Write "holy" on the trunk. Create fruit for each word in the Building Block exercise, and add it to the tree.

HOLDING THE TORAH

Read the paragraph with the students.

Chant the first Hebrew line in unison. Read the English meaning ("Hear…One").

Ask: Why do you think we chant the Sh'ma when we take the Torah from the Ark? (*when we chant the Sh'ma we declare our allegiance to God, whose mitzvot are contained in the Torah; the Sh'ma comes from the Torah [Deuteronomy 6:4]*)

Read the second line in Hebrew and in English.

Ask: How does this second sentence echo the meaning of the Sh'ma? (*like the Sh'ma, it declares that God is One*)

Teach students the melody for this line.

Chant the first two sentences with the students.

Read the third Hebrew sentence.

Reading Rule

Write the word וּנְרוֹמְמָה on the chalkboard. Explain that when a double letter appears in a word and the first letter has a *sh'va* (ְ), *sh'va* is sounded (מְמָ). Call on a student to circle the double letter with the sounded *sh'va* on the chalkboard and have the rest of the class circle the double letter in the text.

Read the English meaning of the third sentence.

Ask: What do the words "acclaim" and "exalt" mean? (*praise, honor, elevate*)

Teach students the melody for this line.

Chant the three sentences with the students.

Discuss the custom of bowing when chanting the third sentence in your synagogue.

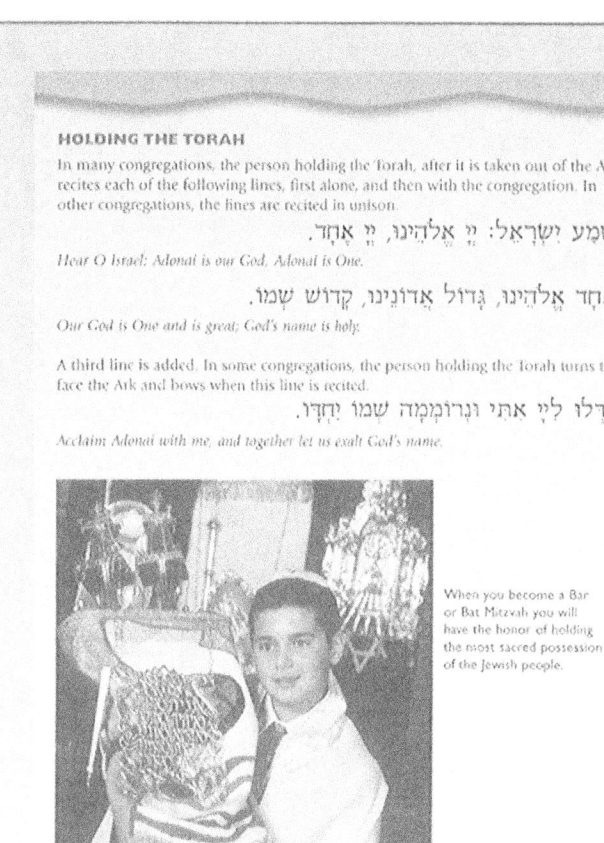

Photo Op

Read the caption to the students. Ask if they have ever been up to the *bimah* and, if so, when. With the permission of the Director of Education or one of the clergy, take students to the sanctuary. Allow each one to hold a *sefer Torah*. Show them how to position the Torah on their shoulders. Allow time for the students to practice walking with the Torah. They'll be surprised how heavy it is!

INTRODUCING לְךָ יְיָ

Read the first paragraph aloud with the students. Ask them to give examples of such exciting experiences from their own lives.

Direct the students to the second paragraph. Ask the following questions:

Why do we stand as the Torah is carried through the congregation? (*to show respect for God and for the Torah*) Why is the Torah carried among the congregants? (*to show it is the Torah of all the people*)

Note: Sometimes congregants show their respect by touching the Torah scroll with the corner of their *tallit* or siddur, which they then bring to their lips. The corners of the *tallit* have *tzitziyot* (singular: *tzitzit*), the knotted fringes which remind us of God's commandments (Numbers 15:37–41).

Read aloud the section below the prayer ("Read the English translation….").

Form *hevruta* groups of two to three students each. Direct groups to discuss the question at the bottom of the page and write their responses on the lines provided. Call on the groups to share their responses.

Have students practice reading the complete prayer in unison, with partners and individually. Teach students the melody for the prayer.

FLUENT READING

Call on students to read each of the following words. Then have students read the complete line.

The word(s) on

- line 1 built on the root "word" (דְּבָרָיו)
- line 2 meaning "Zion" (צִיּוֹן)
- line 3 built on the roots "holy" (קָדְשְׁךָ), "rule" (יִמְלֹךְ), and meaning "Zion" (צִיּוֹן)
- line 4 meaning "Jerusalem" (יְרוּשָׁלָיִם)
- line 5 that is God's name (יְיָ)
- line 6 built on the root "holy" (קִדְּשָׁתּ)
- line 7 meaning "Israel" (יִשְׂרָאֵל)
- line 8 with a *dagesh* that does not change the sound of the letter (הַגָּדוֹל, הַגִּבּוֹר, וְהַנּוֹרָא)
- line 9 meaning "in the Torah" (בַּתּוֹרָה), "and in Moses" (וּבְמֹשֶׁה), and "and in Israel" (וּבְיִשְׂרָאֵל)
- line 10 meaning "Zion" (צִיּוֹן) and "and Jerusalem" (וִירוּשָׁלָיִם)

Letter Perfect

Assign one Hebrew letter to each student, perhaps a letter found in the student's Hebrew name. Have each student find, circle, and read each word in lines 1–10 that contains the assigned letter.

FLUENT READING

Each line below contains a word you know. Practice reading the lines.

1. בָּרוּךְ אַתָּה, יְיָ, הָאֵל הַנֶּאֱמָן בְּכָל דְּבָרָיו.
2. אוֹר חָדָשׁ עַל צִיּוֹן תָּאִיר וְנִזְכֶּה כֻלָּנוּ מְהֵרָה לְאוֹרוֹ.
3. וּבְדִבְרֵי קָדְשְׁךָ כָּתוּב לֵאמֹר: יִמְלֹךְ יְיָ לְעוֹלָם אֱלֹהַיִךְ צִיּוֹן לְדֹר וָדֹר הַלְלוּיָהּ.
4. אִם אֶשְׁכָּחֵךְ יְרוּשָׁלָיִם תִּשְׁכַּח יְמִינִי.
5. גָּדוֹל יְיָ וּמְהֻלָּל מְאֹד וְלִגְדֻלָּתוֹ אֵין חֵקֶר.
6. כִּי בָנוּ בָחַרְתָּ וְאוֹתָנוּ קִדַּשְׁתָּ.
7. רְצֵה יְיָ אֱלֹהֵינוּ בְּעַמְּךָ יִשְׂרָאֵל וּבִתְפִלָּתָם.
8. הָאֵל הַגָּדוֹל הַגִּבּוֹר וְהַנּוֹרָא, אֵל עֶלְיוֹן.
9. בָּרוּךְ אַתָּה, יְיָ, הַבּוֹחֵר בַּתּוֹרָה, וּבְמֹשֶׁה עַבְדּוֹ, וּבְיִשְׂרָאֵל עַמּוֹ, וּבִנְבִיאֵי הָאֱמֶת וָצֶדֶק.
10. לִהְיוֹת עַם חָפְשִׁי בְּאַרְצֵנוּ, אֶרֶץ צִיּוֹן וִירוּשָׁלָיִם.

WORKSHEET

Duplicate and hand out copies of the worksheet for Lesson 2 to review skills and concepts.

FAMILY EDUCATION

Duplicate and send home copies of "As a Family: From Generation to Generation" (at the back of this guide) if you did not do so earlier in the chapter.

LESSON 2
Worksheet

Name: _____

כִּי מִצִּיּוֹן \ לְךָ יְיָ

1. Write the English meaning below each Hebrew word.

   תּוֹרָה   יְרוּשָׁלַיִם   יִשְׂרָאֵל   צִיּוֹן

   _____   _____   _____   _____

2. Unscramble the first sentence of כִּי מִצִּיּוֹן and write the words in the correct order.

   תּוֹרָה כִּי מִירוּשָׁלַיִם מִצִּיּוֹן וּדְבַר יְיָ תֵּצֵא

   _____

3. Why do we carry the Torah up and down the aisles of the congregation before the Torah reading?

   _____
   _____

4. Connect the root to the matching English.

English	Hebrew
speak	קדשׁ
holy	רחמ
make	דבר
mercy	מלכ
rule	עשׂה

5. Name the three days of the week on which the Torah is read.

   _____ _____ _____

6. Explain how Ezra the scribe helped perpetuate the tradition of reading Torah.

   _____
   _____
   _____

LESSON 3
בִּרְכוֹת הַתּוֹרָה

LEARNING OBJECTIVES

Prayer Reading Skills
- The prefix וְ ("and")
- The word ending וֹ ("his")
- The root ברכ ("bless" or "praise")
- Hebrew letters as they appear in the Torah

Prayer Concepts
- We show respect for the Torah by dressing it in fine coverings.
- The Torah is divided into 54 weekly portions called *parashot* or *parashiyot* (singular: *parashah*), which are further divided into readings or sections.
- The yearly cycle of Torah readings begins and ends on Simhat Torah.
- We recite a blessing before and after each section is read.
- The word *aliyah* (plural: *aliyot*) means going up to the *bimah* to recite the two Torah blessings or it means going to live in Israel.
- The number of *aliyot* depends on the day on which the Torah is read.
- Torah terminology: *ba'al k'riah* (m), *ba'alat k'riah* (f); *tikkun*; *trope*; Five Books of Moses; *maftir* (m), *maftirah* (f); *haftarah*; *bimah*; Mi Shebeirach

BEYOND THE TEXTBOOK
Hebrew names

Ritual of *aliyah*

ABOUT THE PRAYER
Each person called to the Torah chants two Torah blessings. The first blessing, recited before the Torah reader begins a section, opens with the Bar'chu, a call to the congregation to praise God. The first blessing then thanks God for choosing the Jewish people to receive the gift of the Torah. The second blessing, recited when the Torah reader completes the section, praises God for giving us the Torah of truth and eternal life.

INSTRUCTIONAL MATERIALS
Text pages 24–35

Word Cards 19–30

Worksheet 3

Family Education: "As a Family: Continuing the Tradition" (at the back of this guide)

SET INDUCTION
Ask: When you give a special gift, how do you hope the receiver will treat the item? (*treasure it, use it well, protect it, pass it on, restore it when necessary*)

Write the following sentences on the chalkboard. Call on students to read each Hebrew sentence and its English meaning.

Kiddush

כִּי בָנוּ בָחַרְתָּ וְאוֹתָנוּ קִדַּשְׁתָּ

You chose us from all the nations and You made us holy.

First Torah Blessing

אֲשֶׁר בָּחַר־בָּנוּ מִכָּל־הָעַמִּים

(God) for choosing us from all the nations and giving us the Torah.

For Discussion
Tell students that the Jewish people traditionally believe they were chosen by God to receive a unique gift, the Torah, but that with this gift come special responsibilities.

Ask: What responsibilities go along with receiving the Torah? (*to fulfill the mitzvot; to live according to the teachings of the Torah*)

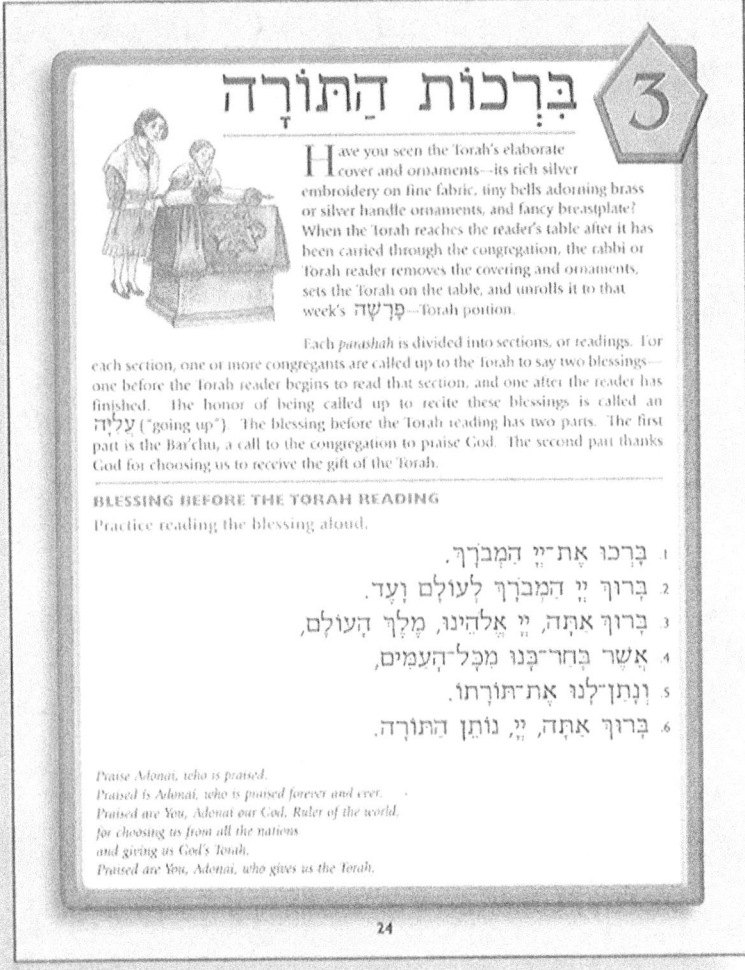

Direct students to read the first three words in line 6 silently. Ask: What do the first three words indicate? (*this is a blessing*) What is the English meaning of the sentence? (*Praised are You…gives us the Torah.*)

Read lines 1–6 in unison with the students.

INTO THE TEXT

Choose students to read aloud the English introduction to the lesson.

Bring in a Jewish calendar. Help students find the name of the Torah portion for that Shabbat.

Your Hebrew Name

We traditionally use the Hebrew name of the person receiving an *aliyah*. We say בֶּן ("son of") or בַּת ("daughter of") after the Hebrew name. We follow בֶּן or בַּת with the parents' Hebrew names; for example, שָׂרָה בַּת יוֹסֵף וְדִינָה. In some congregations, only the father's name is used.

Ask: Why do you think we follow the custom of using the parents' names? (*symbolizes one generation passing the Torah on to the next*)

Ask the students to find out their complete Hebrew names, including their parents' names.

Reading Practice

Direct the students to the first Torah blessing.

Call on individuals to read lines 1 and 2 aloud, then their English meaning. (*Praise Adonai… forever and ever*)

Ask: What is the purpose of these introductory lines in the first blessing?

Hint: Have students reread the second paragraph at the top of the page.

Have students read line 3 silently.

Ask if they recognize the six words. (*the introductory words for a blessing*)

Ask a student to give the English meaning. (*Praised are You…Ruler of the world*)

Have students read lines 4 and 5 aloud.

Ask a student to give the English meaning. (*for choosing us…giving us God's Torah*)

Ask: Why do we praise God for choosing us and giving us the Torah? (*we are proud of the honor; we accept the responsibility to live according to the teachings of the Torah and to pass them on to the next generation*)

MATCH GAME

Allow several minutes for students to complete the activity. Call on individuals to read aloud each Hebrew-English match.

Scrambling

Display Word Cards 19–22 in random order on the edge of the chalkboard. Read aloud the English meaning of each word in the order of the blessing on page 24, line 4. Challenge students to select the matching Word Cards and place them in the correct right-to-left order. Call on students to read the completed phrase: בָּחַר בָּנוּ מִכָּל הָעַמִּים.

Have students close their eyes. Remove one Word Card. Students then open their eyes and read the phrase, including the missing word. Repeat the activity three more times, each time removing one more word until the students "read" the sentence that is "not there."

Display Word Cards 23–25 and repeat each step in this activity.

Photo Op

The Torah mantle—*m'il*—protects the Torah scroll. The mantle has two round openings at the top to allow it to pass over the wooden rollers—the *atzei ḥayim*. Call on a student to read the caption aloud, reading the citation in full: Leviticus, Chapter 25, Verse 10. The quotation on the mantle is from the description in the Torah of the Jubilee Year, which occurs every fiftieth year. "Liberty" referred to the release of slaves, the release of property from mortgages, and the cancellation of all land sales. This is not actually the practice in Israel any longer.

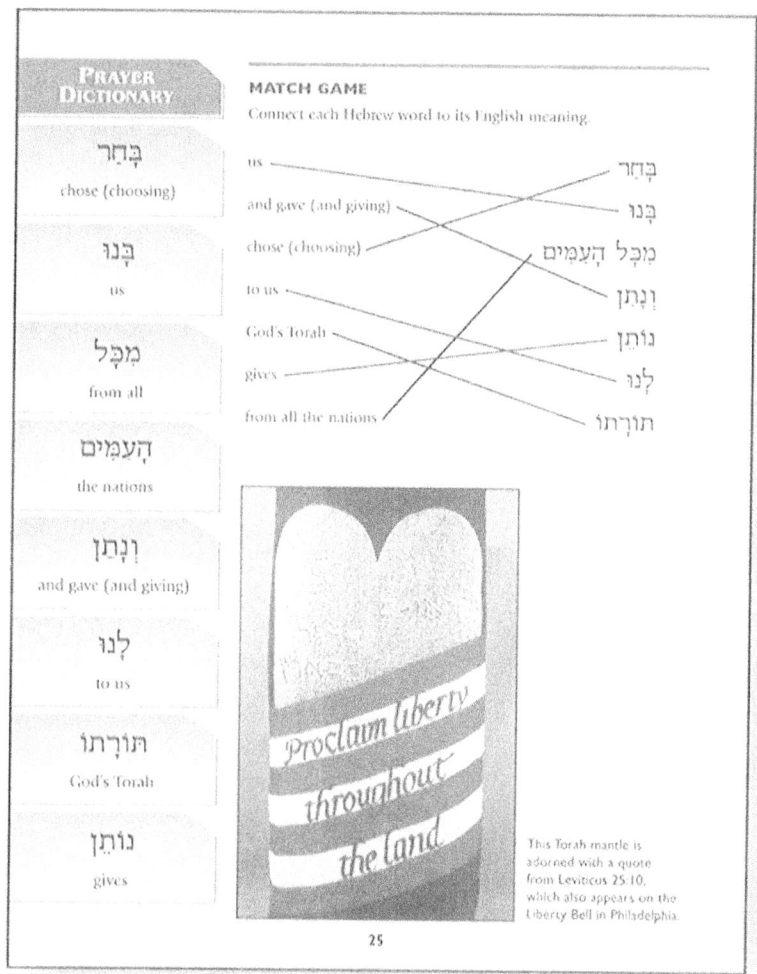

Extending the Opportunity

Discuss the significance of the Liberty Bell in American history and why the quote is appropriate for the bell. (*The Liberty Bell stands in Independence Hall in Philadelphia, Pa. It was rung in July 1776 after the first public reading of the Declaration of Independence, declaring the freedom and liberty of the colonists in their new land.*)

Visit the sanctuary in your synagogue to view the mantles on the Torah scrolls. What is the symbolism of the design on each mantle?

LETTER LINK

Read the explanation with the students.

Direct students to the Torah script in the middle of the page.

Ask: How many letters have crowns? (9) Which letters are they? (ג ז ט נ ן ע צ ץ ש)

Have students connect the matching letters in the four boxes.

Trope Enrichment

Bring a *tikkun* to class so students can see the format. Invite a Torah reader from your synagogue to class to read from both columns in the *tikkun*.

Ask the Torah reader to teach the students some of the trope marks. Allow students the opportunity to read or chant from the *tikkun*.

As a Family

You might wish to send home with students the Family Education page, "As a Family: Continuing the Tradition" at this time.

PRAYER BUILDING BLOCKS

Have the class read lines 1 and 2 at the top of the page.

Tell students to base their responses to the question on earlier class discussions. Direct the students to share their responses.

Learning the Ritual

The person honored with an *aliyah* chants the first line of the Bar'chu. The congregation chants the second line. The honoree repeats the second line and then chants the remaining lines of the Torah blessing. Each person honored with an *aliyah* follows this ritual.

Have the students practice chanting the Torah blessing in this manner.

Read and complete the activity in the middle of the page.

The Fruit of the Tree

Create a fruit tree with the root ברכ. Write "bless" and "praise" on the trunk.

Write the words built on ברכ in the Torah blessing on fruit, and add it to the tree.

אֲשֶׁר בָּחַר בָּנוּ "who chose us" ("for choosing us")

Read and complete the Building Block together with students.

Have students circle the words of the Building Block in line 2 in the middle of the page.

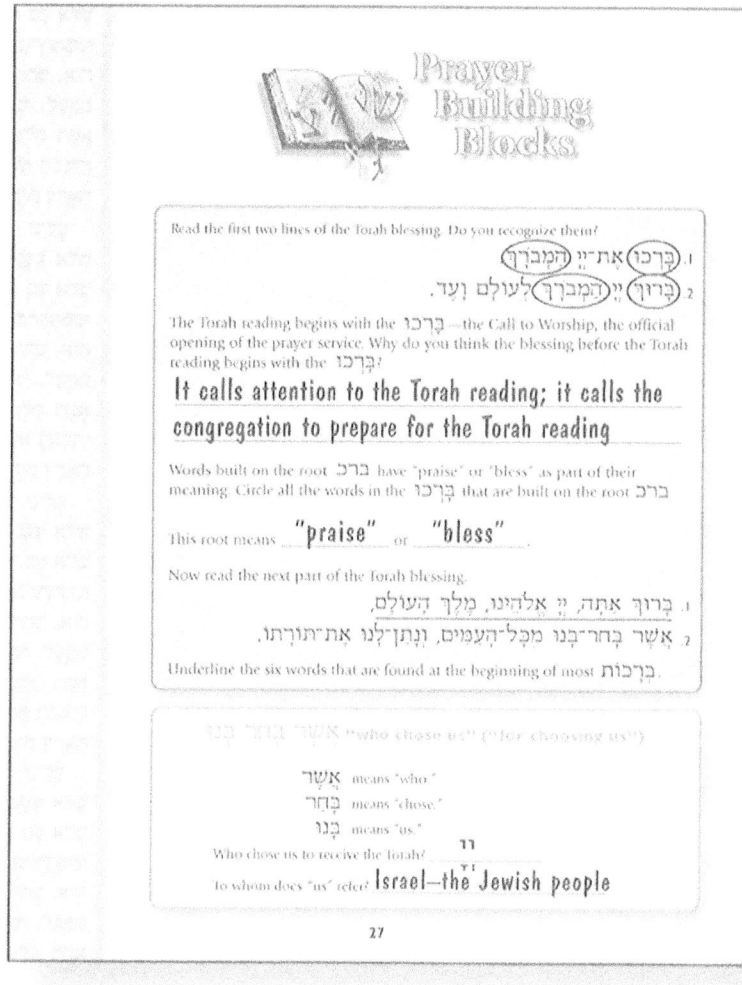

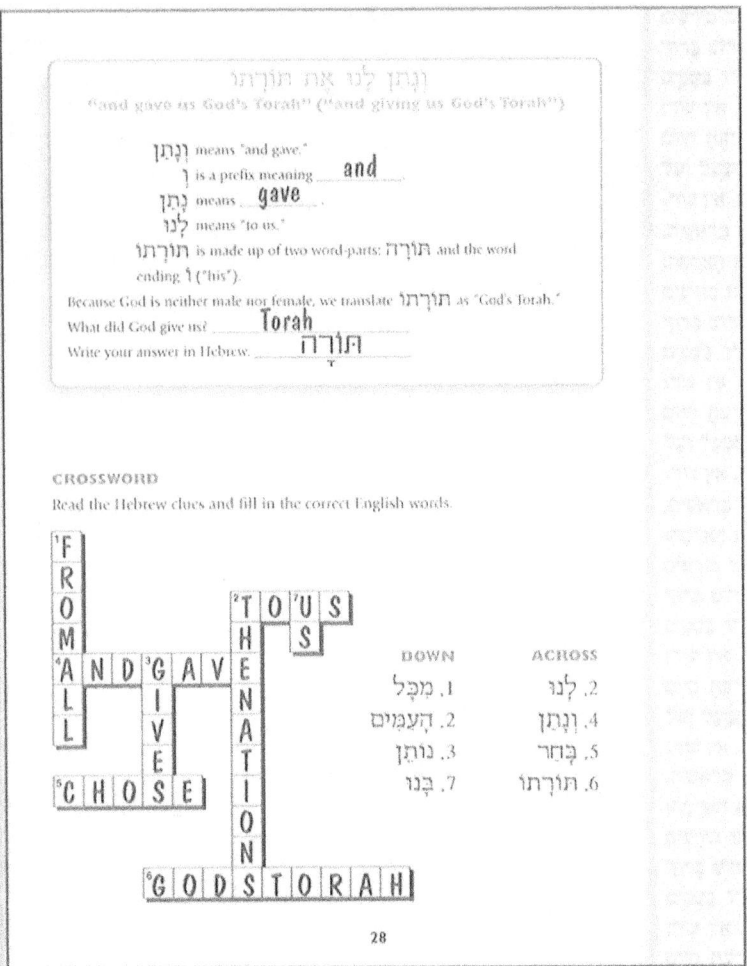

וְנָתַן לָנוּ אֶת תּוֹרָתוֹ
"and gave us God's Torah" ("and giving us God's Torah")

Read and complete the Building Block together with the students.

Have students circle the words of the Building Block in line 2 in the middle of page 27.

Note: We translate תּוֹרָתוֹ as "God's Torah" rather than "His Torah" to indicate that God is neither male nor female.

CROSSWORD

Direct the students to complete the crossword puzzle. They might enjoy working in pairs. Call on students to read their answers aloud: the number, the Hebrew, and then the English.

Extending the Activity

After completing the crossword, students should turn to the blessing on page 24 and read the line with that Hebrew word and the corresponding English line. (Example: 1 Down, מִכָּל, "from all," is found in the blessing on the fourth Hebrew line and the fourth English line.)

Role Play

Designate a student to be honored with an *aliyah*. The class is the congregation. Follow the ritual for chanting the first Torah blessing by reading the complete blessing on page 24.

FACTS AND FIGURES ABOUT THE TORAH READING

Read each fact and figure with the students.

Adding It Up

- The Five Books of Moses are known as the חָמֵשׁ from the Hebrew word חָמֵשׁ ("five").
- The portion of the week is known as פָּרָשַׁת הַשָּׁבוּעַ. The word פָּרָשַׁת means "portion of." הַשָּׁבוּעַ means "week."
- Each פָּרָשַׁת הַשָּׁבוּעַ has a name that is the first important word in the portion.
- The Torah, the Five Books of Moses, is the first section of the Bible.
- The Hebrew name of each of the Five Books is taken from the first important word in the book.

Genesis	בְּרֵאשִׁית
Exodus	שְׁמוֹת
Leviticus	וַיִּקְרָא
Numbers	בְּמִדְבַּר
Deuteronomy	דְּבָרִים

A Review Game

Play one of the games from the "Classroom Games" section in the front of this guide to review facts and figures about the Torah reading.

FACTS AND FIGURES ABOUT THE TORAH READING

- The Torah (also called the Five Books of Moses) is divided into 54 portions (פָּרָשׁוֹת).
- It takes exactly one year to read the whole Torah. We begin reading the first book, Genesis (בְּרֵאשִׁית), on Simhat Torah, and complete reading the last book, Deuteronomy (דְּבָרִים), one year later on the following Simhat Torah. We then begin all over again.
- The last person called to the Torah on Shabbat is known as the *maftir* (for a man or a boy) or the *maftirah* (for a woman or a girl). This is often the Bar Mitzvah or Bat Mitzvah. The *maftir* or *maftirah* recites the blessings before and after the reading of the last few verses of the Torah portion, and then chants a portion from Prophets called the *haftarah*.

Answer the following questions:

1. How many portions (פָּרָשׁוֹת) are contained in the Torah? __54__
2. On which holiday do we finish reading the Torah and begin all over again?
   __Simhat Torah__
3. Explain what the *maftir* or *maftirah* does.
   __The last person called to the Torah on Shabbat;__
   __recites the Torah blessings and chants the haftarah.__
4. How do you think it feels to be the *maftir* or *maftirah*? Why?
   __Special; important; responsible; proud.__
   __It is the highlight of the Torah reading; the climax; it is a__
   __great honor because the *maftir/maftirah* reads the haftarah.__

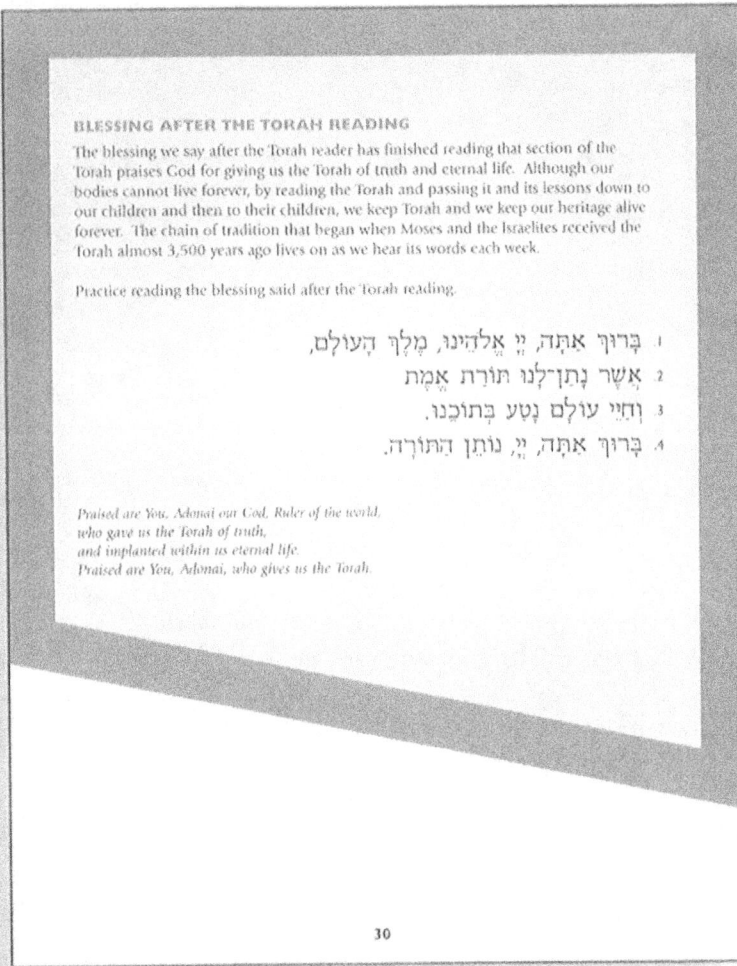

BLESSING AFTER THE TORAH READING

Read the paragraph aloud.

Have the students read the English meaning of the blessing at the bottom of the page. Ask them to explain the theme of the prayer in their own words.

Comparisons: Blessings Before and After the Torah Reading

- Direct students to read the Hebrew blessing.

  Ask: Which two lines are the same as in the blessing before the Torah reading? (*1 and 4*)

- Direct the students to read lines 2 and 3 only.

  Ask: Which of the Hebrew words in the lines do you recognize from the blessing before the Torah reading?

  (אֲשֶׁר נָתַן לָנוּ תּוֹרַת עוֹלָם)

Reading Practice: Blessing After the Torah Reading

Read the complete blessing with the students.

Half and Half

Direct one half of the class, Group A, to the blessing before the Torah reading on page 24.

Direct the other half of the class, Group B, to the blessing after the Torah reading on page 30.

Have Group A read page 24, line 3, and Group B read page 30, line 1, aloud together.

Group A: Have the students read page 24, lines 4 and 5.

Group B: Have the students read page 30, lines 2 and 3.

Call on both groups to read the final line in their Torah blessing aloud together (Group A, page 24, line 6; Group B, page 30, line 4).

PRAYER DICTIONARY

Display Word Cards 27–30. Have students read each Hebrew word in turn. Ask students to give the English meanings for words they know. They may refer to the Prayer Dictionary for meanings of words they do not know.

Display the cards for reading and vocabulary practice.

PHRASE MATCH

Ask the students to cover the Prayer Dictionary to complete the exercise, then uncover it to check their answers. Call on students to read each match aloud.

Photo Op

Read the caption aloud. Ask students to describe what they see in the photograph. Tell them that in the Torah we read, "You shall not put a stumbling block before the blind"—לִפְנֵי עִוֵּר לֹא תִתֵּן מִכְשֹׁל (Leviticus 19:14).

Discuss the *literal* meaning of the mitzvah. (*keep the path clear in front of someone who cannot see*) Then discuss the *underlying* meaning of the mitzvah. (*do not deceive others; do not play upon their weakness; do not prey upon innocent people*)

WHAT'S MISSING?

Display Word Cards 26–30 in random order.

Have all but one student close their books. That student should read aloud the Hebrew in this activity and give the English phrase for the missing part of the sentence.

The other students should determine which of the Word Cards is the correct Hebrew match for the English phrase. ("*Torah of truth,*" Word Cards 27 and 28; "*and eternal life,*" 29 and 30; "*gives,*" 26)

Students may now open their books to page 31 and complete the activity, covering the Prayer Dictionary and the Phrase Match above. They can use the Word Card display to help them complete the activity.

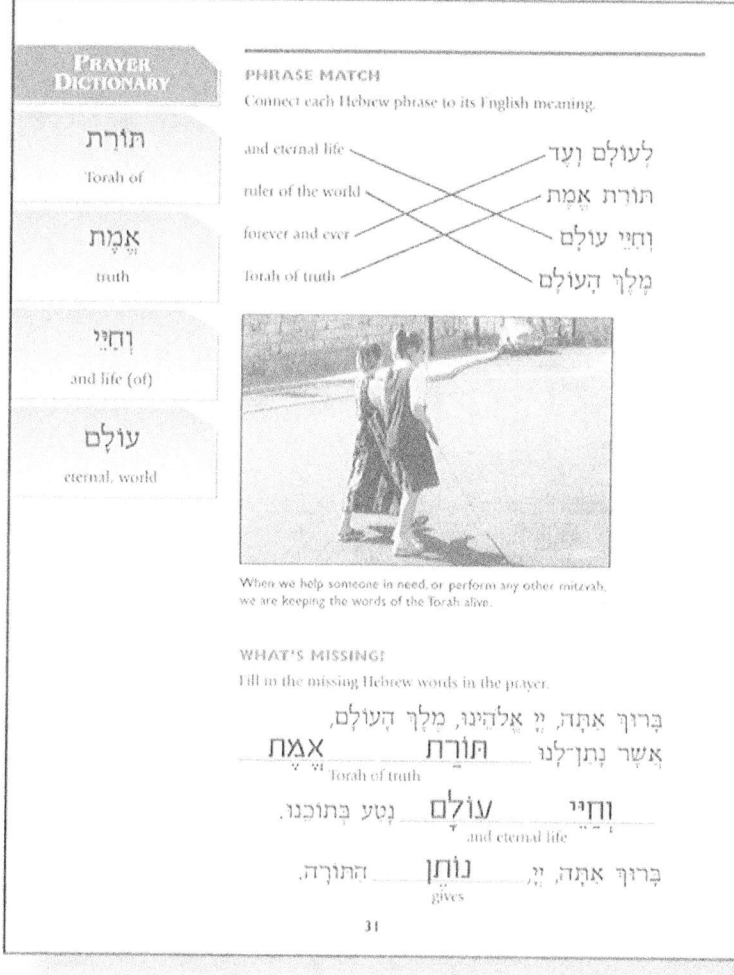

45 LESSON 3

PRAYER BUILDING BLOCKS

אֲשֶׁר נָתַן לָנוּ תּוֹרַת אֱמֶת
"who gave us the Torah of truth"

Complete the Building Block together.

For Discussion

Ask:

- Why do we consider the Torah to be "the truth"? (*it contains God's teachings; we believe in it*)

- Why are the teachings of the Torah a "yardstick" by which we measure our actions? (*it contains the mitzvot; the Torah reflects God's truth; it teaches us how to behave; it is like a guide book for life*)

וְחַיֵּי עוֹלָם "and eternal life"

Complete the Building Block together.

Ask students to interpret the phrase "eternal life." (*although individual Jewish people die every day, the Jewish people as a whole survives and transfers our culture and heritage to each successive generation*)

A Musical Note

Practice chanting the blessings before and after the Torah reading.

עוֹלָם

Have students follow the directions at the top of the page.

Ask: What is the meaning of the word עוֹלָם? (*eternal; forever; world; universe*)

Word Study

- **Final letters.** Call on students to read each word ending with final ם, ן, ך.
- **Dagesh.** Call on students to read each word with a *dagesh* that does not change the sound of the letter in which it is found.
- **Roots.** Call on students to identify words built on the following roots: קדש (line 5); ברכ (lines 3 and 4); מלכ (lines 2 and 6). Challenge students to give the general English meaning of words built on each of these roots. (*holy; bless or praise; rule*)

Line by Line

Divide the students into six groups, one group for each Hebrew line. After they have practiced reading their assigned line, each group should read it in unison. Members can then read the line individually.

CHALLENGE QUESTION

Have the students complete the exercise individually. Call on students to read aloud their response.

Read the following sentences and underline עוֹלָם in each one.

1. וְשִׁבְחֲךָ אֱלֹהֵינוּ מִפִּינוּ לֹא יָמוּשׁ לְעוֹלָם וָעֶד.
2. אֲדוֹן עוֹלָם אֲשֶׁר מָלַךְ בְּטֶרֶם כָּל יְצִיר נִבְרָא.
3. יִתְבָּרַךְ שִׁמְךָ בְּפִי כָּל חַי תָּמִיד לְעוֹלָם וָעֶד.
4. וַאֲנַחְנוּ נְבָרֵךְ יָהּ מֵעַתָּה וְעַד עוֹלָם.
5. נְקַדֵּשׁ אֶת שִׁמְךָ בָּעוֹלָם, כְּשֵׁם שֶׁמַּקְדִּישִׁים אוֹתוֹ בִּשְׁמֵי מָרוֹם.
6. אֵל חַי וְקַיָּם תָּמִיד יִמְלֹךְ עָלֵינוּ לְעוֹלָם וָעֶד.

CHALLENGE QUESTION

Reread the blessing on page 30.

Describe the theme—or main idea—of this blessing, which is recited after the Torah reading.

Torah study is the path to knowing God, which, in turn, leads to one's soul being bound up in the bond of everlasting life; the lessons in the Torah are eternal.

New immigrants making aliyah to the State of Israel

Photo Op

Choose a student to read the caption aloud. Explain that from the late 1800s through 1939, thousands of Jews made *aliyah* to Israel, mainly from eastern Europe. There were many other times in our people's history when immigrants made *aliyah* for freedom and protection. Their countries of origin did not allow Jewish people to live peacefully as full citizens. After World War II, thousands of survivors came to Israel for refuge. Operation Magic Carpet (1949) brought 50,000 Jews suffering poverty from Yemen to Israel. Operation Moses (1984) brought 8,000 Ethiopian Jews suffering from famine to Israel. And in the 1980s and 1990s hundreds of thousands of Jews made *aliyah* from the former Soviet Union to Israel.

ALIYAH

Call on students to read each paragraph. Ask specific questions to confirm students' understanding.

Paragraph 1
- What does "aliyah" mean? (*going up*)
- What is the "bimah"? (*the raised floor for the Ark and the reading table*)
- How does an *aliyah* bring us closer to God? (*we feel close to the Torah and to God both physically and spiritually*)

Paragraph 2
What is the symbolism of "going up" to Israel? (*we are ascending to a higher place spiritually; we are going to the land that God promised the Jewish people in the Torah*)

Paragraph 3
- Why does Shabbat have more *aliyot* than any other day? (*it is holier than all other days*)
- How many *aliyot* are there on Shabbat (*7; even Yom Kippur has fewer—6*)

Paragraph 4
- What is the name of the blessing for well-being? (*Mi Shebeirach*)
- Why do you think we recite a blessing for well-being during the Torah service? (*the Torah service is the highlight of the prayer service; we feel close to God*)

FLUENT READING

Have students search each line for words they know or words built on roots they know.

The Number Game

On individual slips of paper, write the numbers 1–10, one for each line on page 35. (If there are more than ten students, repeat the numbers until there is one for each student.)

Place the papers in a box or bag, or upside down on a table.

Each student should take a slip without looking at the number on it. The student is then responsible for reading the line that corresponds to that number.

Allow a few minutes for reading practice.

Extending the Game:

- Repeat the game and have the students select new numbers. If a student picks the same number as before, he or she should replace it and choose again.
- Have the students pass the number to the person on their right. Each student should then practice and read aloud the new line.

Repeat either option several times to develop fluency in reading.

FLUENT READING

Each line below contains a word you know. Practice reading the lines

1. בָּרוּךְ שֶׁנָּתַן תּוֹרָה לְעַמּוֹ יִשְׂרָאֵל בִּקְדֻשָּׁתוֹ.
2. יְהִי שֵׁם יְיָ מְבֹרָךְ, מֵעַתָּה וְעַד עוֹלָם.
3. הוּא נוֹתֵן לֶחֶם לְכָל בָּשָׂר.
4. תּוֹרָה וּמִצְוֹת, חֻקִּים וּמִשְׁפָּטִים אוֹתָנוּ לִמַּדְתָּ.
5. שֶׁכָּל דְּבָרָיו אֱמֶת וָצֶדֶק.
6. וְתִתֶּן לָנוּ חַיִּים אֲרֻכִּים, חַיִּים שֶׁל שָׁלוֹם, חַיִּים שֶׁל טוֹבָה, חַיִּים שֶׁל בְּרָכָה.
7. כַּכָּתוּב בְּתוֹרָתֶךָ: יְיָ יִמְלֹךְ לְעֹלָם וָעֶד.
8. אֵין לָנוּ מֶלֶךְ אֶלָּא אָתָּה.
9. חַיִּים שֶׁתְּהֵא בָנוּ אַהֲבַת תּוֹרָה וְיִרְאַת שָׁמַיִם.
10. כִּי אַתָּה שׁוֹמֵעַ תְּפִלַּת עַמְּךָ יִשְׂרָאֵל.

WORKSHEET

Duplicate and hand out the worksheet for Lesson 3 to review skills and concepts.

FAMILY EDUCATION

Duplicate and send home copies of "As a Family: Continuing the Tradition" (at the back of this guide) if you have not already done so.

LESSON 3
Worksheet

Name: _____

בִּרְכוֹת הַתּוֹרָה

1. What is the name of the first part of the blessing before the Torah reading? Choose your answer from the words below.

   _____

   שְׁמַע   בָּרְכוּ   עֲשֵׂה שָׁלוֹם

2. Why does this prayer introduce the blessing before the Torah reading?

   _____

3. The following phrases are part of the blessing before the Torah reading. Number them in the correct order, using the English translation below as your guide.

   ☐ אֶת תּוֹרָתוֹ   ☐ מִכָּל הָעַמִּים
   ☐ אֲשֶׁר בָּחַר בָּנוּ   ☐ וְנָתַן לָנוּ

   for choosing us from all the nations and giving us God's Torah

4. The following phrases are part of the blessing after the Torah reading. Number them in the correct order, using the English translation below as your guide.

   ☐ אֲשֶׁר נָתַן לָנוּ   ☐ וְחַיֵּי עוֹלָם
   ☐ נָטַע בְּתוֹכֵנוּ   ☐ תּוֹרַת אֱמֶת

   who gave us the Torah of truth, and implanted within us eternal life

5. Explain the meaning of these Torah terms.

   עֲלִיָּה _____

   פָּרָשָׁה _____

   בַּעַל\בַּעֲלַת קְרִיאָה _____

   מִי שֶׁבֵּרַךְ _____

6. On which holiday do we finish reading the Torah and begin all over again?

   _____

LESSON 4
בִּרְכוֹת הַהַפְטָרָה

LEARNING OBJECTIVES

Prayer Reading Skills
- The prefixes בְּ ("in"); הַ הָ ("the"); וּ וְ ("and")
- The word ending וֹ ("his")
- The plural ending ים (masc.)
- The roots אמר ("speak" or "say"); בחר ("choose")

Prayer Concepts
- תָּנָ״ךְ is the Hebrew acronym for "Bible." It represents the three parts of the Bible, תּוֹרָה, נְבִיאִים, כְּתוּבִים—Torah, Prophets, Writings.
- Haftarah means "conclusion."
- The haftarah is a reading from נְבִיאִים (Prophets).
- The blessing before the haftarah reading praises God for the prophets, who spread the words of the Torah to the Jewish people.
- The trope melodies for reading the Torah and the haftarah are different.
- Ethical Echoes: אֱמֶת ("truth"), צְדָקָה ("righteousness" or "justice")

BEYOND THE TEXTBOOK

Reading Rules:
- The double-duty dot (מֹשֶׁה)
- The "eye" ending, אָיו; the "ahv" ending, אָיו

The roots אמן ("faithful"); דבר ("speak," "word," or "thing")

The term אָמֵן

The ritual of the *maftir aliyah*

ABOUT THE PRAYER

The haftarah is a reading from *N'vi'im*, the second section of the Bible. The prophets were spokespersons for God. They lived and preached over a period of 750 years—from the time the people of Israel entered Canaan, the Promised Land, around 1250 BCE, until the time of their return from exile in Babylon in 538 BCE. The prophets brought hope to the people in times of despair. When the people strayed from the teachings of the Torah, the prophets chastised them and led them back to God and the mitzvot.

There are five blessings that accompany the haftarah reading—one before the reading and four after the reading. Each blessing reflects traditional aspects of our relationship with God.

INSTRUCTIONAL MATERIALS

Text pages 36–45

Word Cards 19, 31–38

Worksheet 4

Family Education: "As a Family: Telling the Truth" (at the back of this guide)

SET INDUCTION

Ask students to think about people in their lives who have taught them a valuable life lesson or skill. What qualities do they admire in that person?

Before class, prepare a bulletin board or wall display with the heading נְבִיאִים, Prophets. Explain that the prophets lived thousands of years ago and taught the people how to treat each other with justice and mercy. Those lessons are timeless.

Hand each student an index card with the name of a prophet written in bold print in both Hebrew and English. (Use the names given below.) Read aloud the Hebrew and English names of the prophets, directing students, in turn, to add the name of their prophet to the display when they hear it called.

Prophets: יְהוֹשֻׁעַ (Joshua), דְּבוֹרָה (Deborah), יְשַׁעְיָהוּ (Isaiah), יִרְמְיָהוּ (Jeremiah), יְחֶזְקֵאל (Ezekiel), הוֹשֵׁעַ (Hosea), יוֹאֵל (Joel), עָמוֹס (Amos), עוֹבַדְיָה (Obadiah), יוֹנָה (Jonah), מִיכָה (Micah), נַחוּם (Nahum), חֲבַקּוּק (Habakkuk), צְפַנְיָה (Zephaniah), חַגַּי (Haggai), זְכַרְיָה (Zechariah), מַלְאָכִי (Malachi).

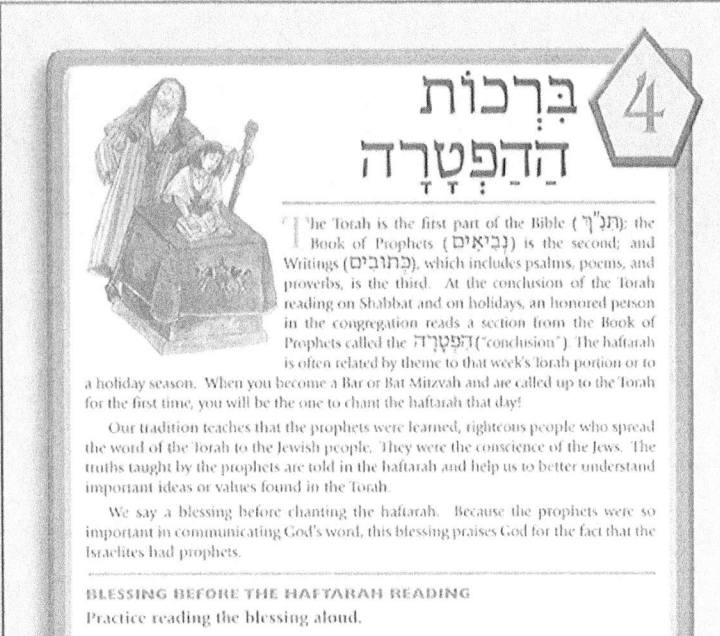

INTO THE TEXT

Direct students to the introduction to the chapter at the top of the page.

Call on students to read the first paragraph aloud. Review the role of the *maftir* (*maftirah*, fem.) on page 29. Explain that *maftir* means "the one who concludes" or "the one who reads the haftarah."

Call on a student to read the second paragraph. Ask what it means to be "the conscience of the Jews." (*the voice that tells them how to behave properly*)

Call on a student to read the third paragraph.

Direct students to the English translation of the blessing before the haftarah reading.

What qualities of the prophets are highlighted in the blessing? (*goodness; faithfulness; truthfulness; righteousness*)

Extending the Concept

Ask: What is the relationship between God, Torah, Moses, and Israel? (*Moses, a prophet chosen by God, communicated the words of the Torah to the people of Israel, who accepted the Torah and passed it down throughout the generations.*)

Reading Practice

Write the word נְבִיאִים ("prophets") on the chalkboard. Ask students to read:

Sentence 1 (lines 1–2):

- the word related to נְבִיאִים (בִּנְבִיאִים)
- the word built on the root דבר (בְּדִבְרֵיהֶם, "with their words")
- the whole sentence

Sentence 2 (lines 3–4):

- the word related to נְבִיאִים (וּבִנְבִיאֵי)
- the words meaning "in the Torah" (בַּתּוֹרָה), "and in Moses" (וּבְמֹשֶׁה), and "and in Israel" (וּבְיִשְׂרָאֵל)
- the whole sentence

Enrichment

As you teach this chapter, you might read selections from Prophets. In each case, have students consider how this "teaching" could affect their lives. Suggested readings: Malachi 2:10; Zachariah 8:16; Isaiah 58:6–8; Amos 5:24; Micah 6:8; Jeremiah 22:13–16.

PRAYER DICTIONARY

- Call on nine students to each read one Hebrew word in the Prayer Dictionary. After each word is read, the class should read the English meaning.
- Call on nine students to stand in random order and display Word Cards 19, 31–38 with the English side facing the class. Have nine other students each read one of the English meanings on display (example: "in truth"). The student holding that card should turn it over to show the Hebrew side, and read the Hebrew word (בֶּאֱמֶת) aloud. Continue until all nine Hebrew words are facing the class.
- Repeat the game, this time starting with the Hebrew side of the cards facing the class.

THE FAMILY CONNECTION

Have the students complete the exercise independently. Call on them to read aloud each set of Hebrew words and the English meaning.

Direct the students to lightly circle each Family Connection word in the blessing on page 36. (Word Set 1: lines 1 and 3; Word Set 2: lines 2 and 4; Word Set 3: lines 2 and 4) Call on individual students to read in the blessing the complete phrase that contains a circled word. A phrase may be read more than once; for example, אֲשֶׁר בָּחַר בִּנְבִיאִים טוֹבִים contains both בִּנְבִיאִים and בָּחַר.

Photo Op

Call on a student to read the caption for the photograph. Ask students when each one will turn thirteen (for boys) or twelve (for girls) and celebrate becoming a Bar or Bat Mitzvah. Discuss that the rabbis considered that, in general, age thirteen for boys and twelve for girls was the age of physical maturity. Pirke Avot 5:24 tells us that at age thirteen a boy is responsible for doing mitzvot. During the thirteenth and fourteenth centuries, the tradition of calling a boy to the Torah to chant the blessings, the Torah portion, and the haftarah was established. In 1921, the first girl had a public ceremony acknowledging her becoming a Bat Mitzvah. She was Judith Kaplan, daughter of Mordecai Kaplan, founder of the Reconstructionist Movement.

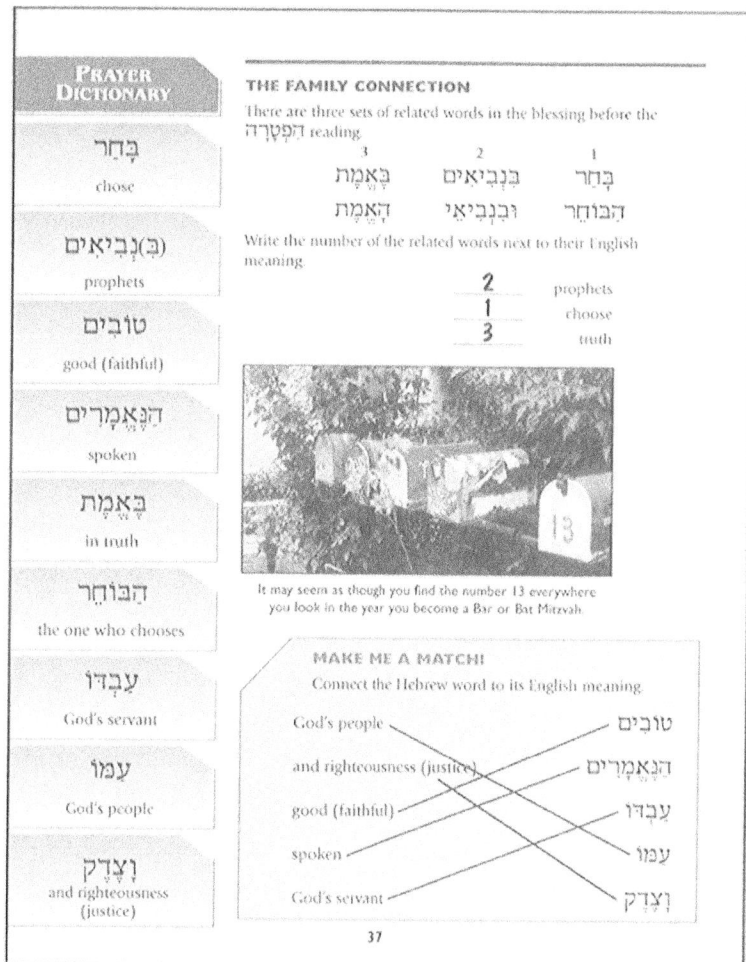

MAKE ME A MATCH!

Have the students cover the Prayer Dictionary and complete the exercise, then uncover it to check their answers. Have them read each match aloud.

53   LESSON 4

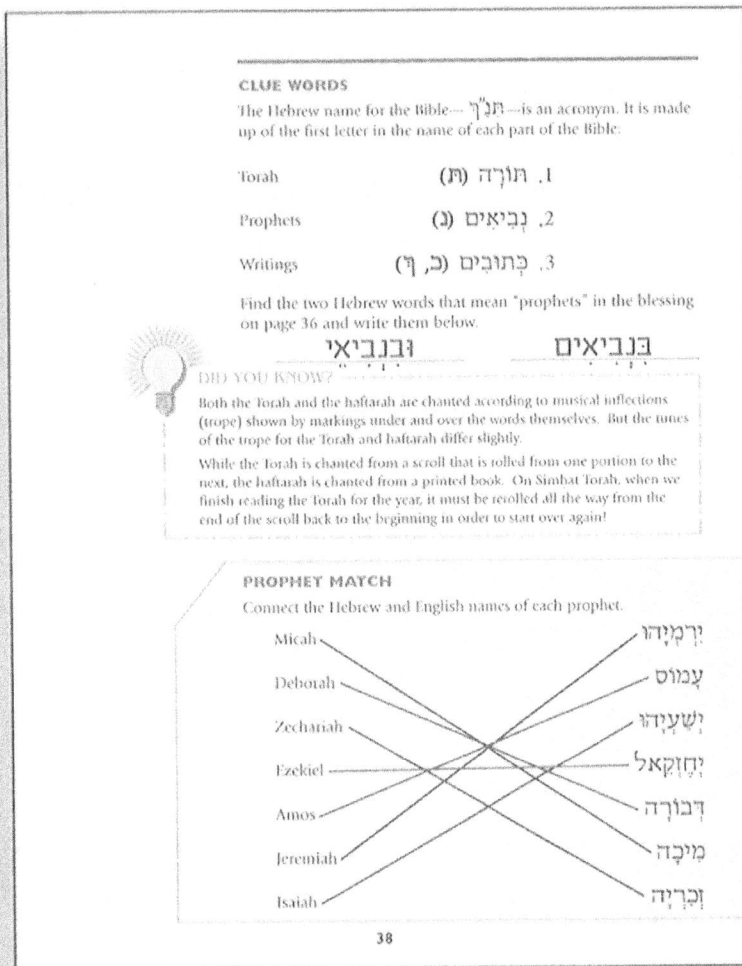

Background

The books of the early prophets tell the history of our people from their entry into the Promised Land under Joshua's leadership to the destruction of Jerusalem more than 500 years later. These are the books of Joshua, Judges, Samuel I and II, and Kings I and II.

The books of the later prophets record their attempts to bring the people back to God and to bring them comfort after the destruction of Jerusalem in 586 BCE, and the exile to Babylon. These books include the major prophets Isaiah, Jeremiah, and Ezekiel and the twelve minor prophets, including Hosea, Amos, and Malachi. The latter are known as "minor" not because their message is unimportant, but because each of their books is quite short.

CLUE WORDS

Explain to students that they will read about an acronym—a word formed from the first letters of a phrase or series of related words. (Examples: NATE—National Association of Temple Educators; NASA—National Aeronautical Space Administration)

Read the section aloud with students.

Direct students' attention to the first letter in each Hebrew word in Clue Words:

תּוֹרָה נְבִיאִים כְּתוּבִים

Remind students that the letter כ changes to its final form at the end of a word. כ becomes ך in the word תַּנַ״ךְ.

Instruct the students to complete the activity. Call on individuals to read each Hebrew phrase on page 36 that contains the word meaning "prophets."
(lines 1–2: אֲשֶׁר בָּחַר בִּנְבִיאִים טוֹבִים;
line 4: וּבְנִבִיאֵי הָאֱמֶת וָצֶדֶק)

DID YOU KNOW?

Read the section aloud with students.

Bring in ḥumashim and distribute to the class. Ask students to open the ḥumashim to a haftarah passage and point out the variety of trope marks. Mention that they are the same markings as those for Torah trope, but the melodies differ. (See Chapter 3, page 26.)

If your students know how to chant trope, encourage them to read and then chant a verse.

PROPHET MATCH

Allow students several minutes to complete the exercise independently. Then call on individuals to read the matches aloud.

Ask if anyone in the class has the same Hebrew name as a prophet.

PRAYER BUILDING BLOCKS

אֲשֶׁר בָּחַר בִּנְבִיאִים טוֹבִים
"who chose good (faithful) prophets"

Call on the students to read the Building Block phrase aloud.

Point out that the end יִם ָ indicates the plural form of a masculine word. Remind students that Hebrew nouns are either masculine or feminine. When a noun is plural, for example, בִּנְבִיאִים ("prophets"), the adjective is also plural, for example, טוֹבִים ("good").

Direct students to complete the Building Block independently and then to share their answers.

הַנֶּאֱמָרִים בֶּאֱמֶת "spoken in truth"

Call on students to read the Building Block phrase aloud.

Direct them to complete the Building Block independently and then to share their answers.

Thumbs Up

Play the following game with the students.

Warm-Up: Ask students to read the circled words built on the root אמר (lines 1–5) in unison and individually.

Play: Each student should select, practice, and read aloud two of the five lines. For each line a student reads correctly, he or she can give the "thumbs up" sign.

The Fruit of the Tree

Create a fruit tree with the root אמר. Write "speak" and "say" on the trunk. Add fruit using the Building Block word (הַנֶּאֱמָרִים) and the circled words in lines 1–5.

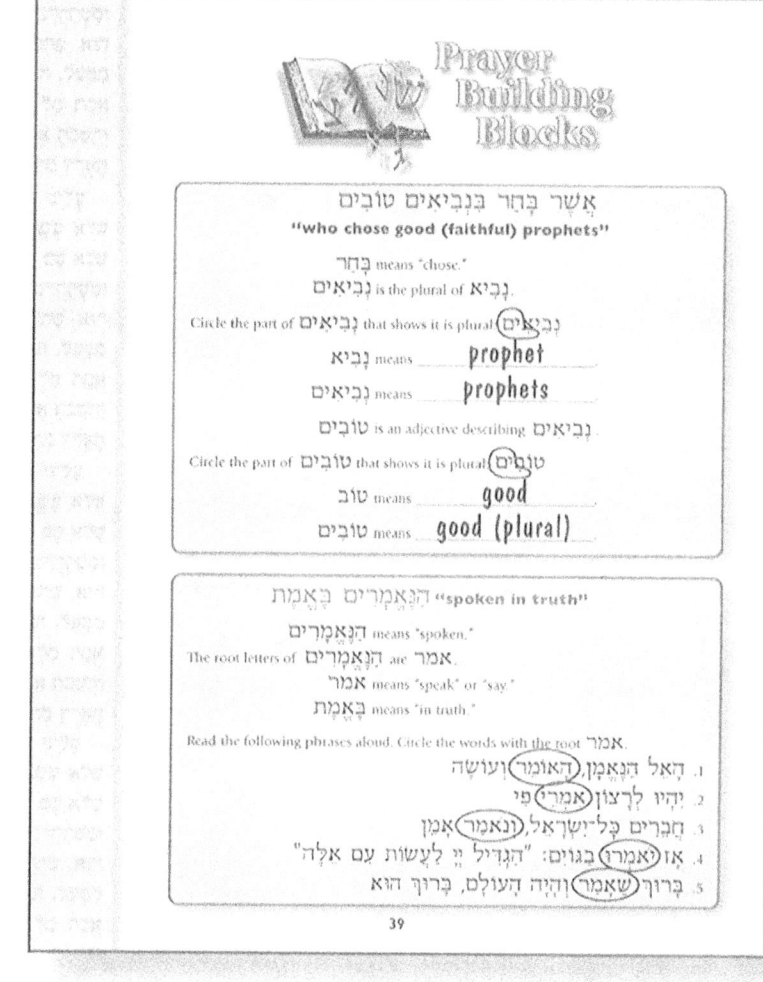

55   LESSON 4

Reproduction of student page (left)

An Ethical Echo

Psalm 15 teaches us that telling the truth—אֱמֶת—is so important that only those who "speak truth in their hearts and have no slander on their tongues" will "live in God's house." The prophets, whose words we read in the haftarah, were also known as "prophets of truth," because they passed the truth of righteous and just behavior from God to the Jewish people.

Think About This!

It would be hard to find someone who's *never* told a lie! Maybe you ate a slice of the freshly baked apple pie meant for that night's dinner guests, and then pretended it wasn't you. Perhaps you forgot to walk the dog, but then claimed you did, so your dad wouldn't get upset. Or maybe you've joined in spreading false rumors about someone. What does the expression "to get caught in a web of lies" mean? In addition to being truthful to others, why do we need to be truthful to ourselves?

הַבּוֹחֵר בַּתּוֹרָה "the one who chooses the Torah"

הַבּוֹחֵר means "the one who chooses."
In this phrase, הַ is a prefix meaning "the one who."
בּוֹחֵר means **chooses**
הַבּוֹחֵר is built on the root בחר
The root בחר tells us that "choose" is part of a word's meaning.

Below are lines from two prayers you have studied. Read each excerpt and circle all the words built on the root בחר. Then write the number of the line from each prayer next to the name of the prayer.

1. בָּרוּךְ אַתָּה, יְיָ אֱלֹהֵינוּ, מֶלֶךְ הָעוֹלָם, אֲשֶׁר (בָּחַר) בָּנוּ מִכָּל־הָעַמִּים, וְנָתַן־לָנוּ אֶת־תּוֹרָתוֹ.

2. כִּי בָנוּ (בָחַרְתָּ) וְאוֹתָנוּ קִדַּשְׁתָּ מִכָּל הָעַמִּים.

Kiddush **#2**
Blessing Before the Torah Reading **#1**

40

AN ETHICAL ECHO

Read the paragraph aloud with the students.

Explain that the Book of Psalms is found in Writings, כְּתוּבִים, the third section of the Bible.

Pose the following questions:

- What does it mean to "speak the truth in your heart"? (*to be honest with yourself; to know what is right and live accordingly; to speak the truth out loud too*)

- What does "slander on their tongues" mean? (*talking ill of others; demeaning others; gossiping; making up stories about others*)

THINK ABOUT THIS!

Read this section aloud with the students.

Ask students:

- What happens to insects that get caught in a spider's web? (*cannot extricate themselves; the more they struggle, the more entangled they get*)

- Why is it hard to untangle yourself from a "web of lies"? (*the lie is carried from one person to another and is hard to undo; the lie leads to other lies*)

- What does it mean to be truthful to yourself? (*not to deceive yourself and pretend something is so when it isn't; to be honest with yourself*)

הַבּוֹחֵר בַּתּוֹרָה
"the one who chooses the Torah"

Call on a student to read the Building Block phrase aloud.

Complete the Building Block with the students.

Challenge: Ask students to give the English meaning of each line. (*line 1: Praised are You, Adonai our God, Ruler of the world, for choosing us from all the nations and giving us God's Torah; line 2: You chose us from all the nations and made us holy*)

Note: You may wish to explain to students that the traditional belief is that God chose the Jewish people for special responsibilities, such as doing mitzvot.

וּבְמֹשֶׁה עַבְדּוֹ
"and Moses, God's servant"

Call on a student to read the Building Block phrase aloud.

Reading Rule: Double-Duty Dot

The dot in the name מֹשֶׁה (מֹשׁ) serves two purposes:

- It is the "oh" vowel for the letter מֹ.
- It indicates the letter שׁ.

Complete the Building Block together.

Discuss responses to the question at the end of the Building Block.

Photo Op

Call on a student to read the caption aloud.

Introduce the phrase *l'shon hara* ("the evil tongue"). Ask students to explain the phrase. (*gossiping; telling lies; spreading rumors; doing harm with words*)

Introduce the phrase *sh'mirat halashon* ("guarding your tongue"). Ask students to explain the phrase. (*being careful what you say; holding your tongue; not talking badly about others*)

וּבְיִשְׂרָאֵל עַמּוֹ
"and Israel, God's people"

Call on a student to read the Building Block phrase aloud.

Complete the Building Block together.

Making Connections

Read aloud the following sentences from the Building Blocks on page 41.

1. Because God is neither male nor female, we translate עַבְדּוֹ as "God's servant."
2. Because God is neither male nor female, we translate עַמּוֹ as "God's people."

Ask:
- What is the common ending for each word, עַמּוֹ and עַבְדּוֹ? (וֹ)
- What does this ending mean? (*his*)
- Why do we not say "His servant" or "His people?" ("*His,*" *although grammatically correct, would indicate that God is male. God has no form—either male or female.*)

LESSON 4

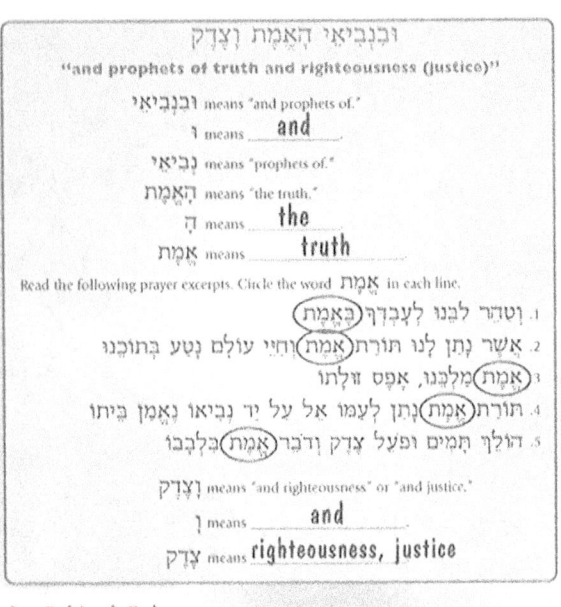

וּבִנְבִיאֵי הָאֱמֶת וָצֶדֶק
"and prophets of truth and righteousness (justice)"

Call on a student to read the Building Block phrase aloud.

Complete the first part of the Building Block with the students.

High Five

Call on individual students to read lines 1–5 aloud as follows:

The reader rests his or her elbow on the desk with the arm held upward and the hand in a light fist. Each time a line is read correctly, the reader raises one finger until he or she makes a high five. (Example: Line 1: thumb; line 2: pointer finger; and so on until all the fingers are raised and the palm shows a high five.)

AN ETHICAL ECHO

Read the paragraph aloud with the class.

Read from Isaiah 58:5–7, 10. In these verses God, speaking through Isaiah, tells the people they should fast "to let the oppressed go free…share your bread with the hungry…then your light shall shine in the darkness.…"

Ask: What is the meaning of the phrase "then your light shall shine in the darkness"? (*light represents hope, darkness represents despair; acts of tzedakah bring hope into the lives of those afflicted by oppression and hunger*)

THINK ABOUT THIS!

Discuss each question with the students. (*giving food or clothing are acts of tzedakah; the highest level of tzedakah is helping a person to become self-sufficient and self-supporting; giving anonymously saves the recipient from embarrassment and does not require thanks; we give tzedakah for its own sake*)

BLESSINGS AFTER THE HAFTARAH READING

Read the first paragraph with the students. Encourage them to talk about times in their own lives when they counted on someone and that person came through.

Read the second and third paragraphs with the students.

Direct students to the first blessing after the haftarah. This blessing speaks of the "faithful God." Have students circle the word "faithful" in their texts each time it appears in the English translation of the prayer. Call on individual students to read each English phrase. (*the faithful God; You are faithful; and faithful are Your words; for You are a faithful and compassionate God and Ruler; faithful in all Your words*)

Prayer Study

Write the root אמנ ("faithful") on the chalkboard.

Have students find and circle each word built on the root אמנ in lines 2, 4, 5, and 7.
(הַנֶּאֱמָן, נֶאֱמָן, וְנֶאֱמָנִים, נֶאֱמָן, הַנֶּאֱמָן)

Call on students to read each phrase that contains a circled word.

Amen

Explain that the word אָמֵן means "so be it." אָמֵן is built on the root אמנ.

Ask: What is the significance of saying אָמֵן at the conclusion of a blessing? (*you have faith that the words are true; you agree with the words of the blessing; you acknowledge another person having said the blessing and do not have to repeat it yourself*)

The Fruit of the Tree

Create a fruit tree with the root אמנ. Write "faithful" on the trunk. Add fruit using words built on the root אמנ.

Reading Rule Review

When the vowel ָ is followed by a *yud* (י), it has the sound "eye" (אַי). When the letter ו follows the ending sound "eye," the ending has the sound "ahv" (אָיו). Write the word דְּבָרָיו on the chalkboard for students to practice reading.

Root Review

Write the root דבר ("speak," "word," or "thing") on the chalkboard.

Have the students find and read each phrase in lines 3–7 that contains a word built on the root דבר. Add fruit with these words to the דבר tree.
(הַמְדַבֵּר, דְּבָרָיו, דְּבָרֶיךָ, וְדָבָר, מִדְּבָרֶיךָ, דְּבָרָיו)

Righteous and Just

Have the students find and read each phrase in lines 2–3 that contains a word meaning "righteous" or "just." (צַדִּיק, וָצֶדֶק)

Chanting Skills

Teach students to chant the first blessing after the haftarah.

> **BLESSINGS GALORE!**
>
> You learned that the blessing before the haftarah praises God for choosing prophets who are faithful, who speak the truth, and who act justly.
>
> The four blessings after the haftarah have very different themes. Read the theme for each blessing, then answer the question.
>
> Blessing 1
> praises God, whose words are true and who fulfills all promises.
>
> Blessing 2
> asks God to have mercy on and to protect Zion, and prays for our return there. In ancient times, Zion was another name for Jerusalem.
>
> Blessing 3
> asks God to reinstate the descendants of David as the rulers of the Jewish people.
>
> Blessing 4
> thanks God for: (1) the Torah, (2) the worship service, (3) the prophets, and (4) Shabbat, our holy day of rest.
>
> How is the fourth blessing after the haftarah the high point of all the other blessings, including the blessing before the haftarah?
>
> **The combination of Torah study, prayer, allegiance to the lessons of the prophets, and Shabbat observance together are the key to preserving the Jewish people.**
>
> **DID YOU KNOW?**
> We are not sure exactly when the הַפְטָרָה blessings were composed. The *Amoraim*—the rabbis whose commentaries on Jewish law are recorded in the *Gemara*—first referred to these blessings around the year 300 C.E. So the haftarah blessings are at least 1,700 years old.
>
> 44

BLESSINGS GALORE!

Call on individual students to read aloud the themes of the four blessings after the haftarah.

Before students fill in the answer to the question, discuss it together. (*the combination of Torah study, prayer, allegiance to the lessons of the prophets, and Shabbat observance together are the key to preserving the Jewish people*)

DID YOU KNOW?

Read the paragraph aloud with the students.

Note: The Mishnah and *Gemara* together make up the Talmud, the post-biblical rabbinic and scholarly writings on the Torah. The Talmud was probably completed in the fifth to sixth centuries CE.

Ask: Why do *you* think there are five haftarah blessings? Discuss individual responses.

Tell students that commentators have noted that if you add the five haftarah blessings to the two Torah blessings, you get a total of seven blessings. Seven represents Shabbat, the seventh day. Seven is also the number of *aliyot* on Shabbat.

Rituals

Remind students of the following rituals:

- The *maftir* (*maftirah*, fem.) is called to the Torah to recite the blessings before and after the last section of the Torah portion is read. This is known as the *maftir aliyah*.
- Following the *maftir aliyah*, members of the congregation are called to the *bimah* to lift the Torah (*hagbahah*) and to dress the Torah (*g'lilah*).
- The *maftir* then chants the blessing before the reading of the haftarah.
- The *maftir* chants the haftarah.
- Following the haftarah, the *maftir* chants four more blessings.
- The *maftir* or *maftirah* is often the young man or woman becoming Bar or Bat Mitzvah.

FLUENT READING

Blessing II
Vocabulary Recognition

Ask: Which word means "Zion"? (צִיּוֹן) Have students circle צִיּוֹן in lines 1 and 2.

Call on students to read aloud each phrase containing the word צִיּוֹן. (line 1: first phrase; line 2: last phrase)

What does צִיּוֹן represent? (*Jerusalem; all of Israel*)

Read the second line and then the complete blessing in unison with the students.

Call on individual students to read the blessing.

Blessing III
Vocabulary Recognition

Ask students:

Which phrase in line 3 means "with Elijah the prophet"? (בְּאֵלִיָּהוּ הַנָּבִיא)

What is the meaning of the last phrase in line 6? (*Shield of David*)

Read the last line and then the complete blessing in unison with the students.

Call on individual students to read the blessing.

Blessing IV
Vocabulary Recognition

Ask students to read the phrase meaning: "for the Torah" (עַל־הַתּוֹרָה); "and for the worship" (וְעַל־הָעֲבוֹדָה); "and for the prophets" (וְעַל־הַנְּבִיאִים); "and for this Sabbath day" (וְעַל־יוֹם הַשַּׁבָּת הַזֶּה)

Ask students to read the words built on the root for:

* "holy" in lines 8 and 11 (לְקַדְּשָׁהּ, מְקַדֵּשׁ)
* "bless" or "praise" in lines 9–11
  (וּמְבָרְכִים, יִתְבָּרַךְ, בָּרוּךְ)

Read the last line and then the complete blessing in unison with the students.

Call on individual students to read the blessing.

FLUENT READING

Practice reading blessings two, three, and four which are said after the הַפְטָרָה reading.

II
1. רַחֵם עַל־צִיּוֹן כִּי הִיא בֵּית חַיֵּינוּ, וְלַעֲלוּבַת נֶפֶשׁ תּוֹשִׁיעַ
2. בִּמְהֵרָה בְיָמֵינוּ. בָּרוּךְ אַתָּה, יְיָ, מְשַׂמֵּחַ צִיּוֹן בְּבָנֶיהָ.

III
3. שַׂמְּחֵנוּ, יְיָ אֱלֹהֵינוּ, בְּאֵלִיָּהוּ הַנָּבִיא עַבְדֶּךָ, וּבְמַלְכוּת בֵּית דָּוִד
4. מְשִׁיחֶךָ, בִּמְהֵרָה יָבֹא וְיָגֵל לִבֵּנוּ. עַל־כִּסְאוֹ לֹא־יֵשֵׁב זָר
5. וְלֹא־יִנְחֲלוּ עוֹד אֲחֵרִים אֶת־כְּבוֹדוֹ, כִּי בְשֵׁם קָדְשְׁךָ נִשְׁבַּעְתָּ
6. לּוֹ שֶׁלֹּא־יִכְבֶּה נֵרוֹ לְעוֹלָם וָעֶד. בָּרוּךְ אַתָּה, יְיָ, מָגֵן דָּוִד.

IV
7. עַל־הַתּוֹרָה, וְעַל־הָעֲבוֹדָה, וְעַל הַנְּבִיאִים, וְעַל־יוֹם הַשַּׁבָּת הַזֶּה,
8. שֶׁנָּתַתָּ־לָּנוּ, יְיָ אֱלֹהֵינוּ, לִקְדֻשָּׁה וְלִמְנוּחָה, לְכָבוֹד וּלְתִפְאָרֶת,
9. עַל־הַכֹּל, יְיָ אֱלֹהֵינוּ, אֲנַחְנוּ מוֹדִים לָךְ, וּמְבָרְכִים אוֹתָךְ.
10. יִתְבָּרַךְ שִׁמְךָ בְּפִי כָּל־חַי תָּמִיד לְעוֹלָם וָעֶד.
11. בָּרוּךְ אַתָּה, יְיָ, מְקַדֵּשׁ הַשַּׁבָּת.

WORKSHEET

Duplicate and hand out copies of the worksheet for Lesson 4 to review skills and concepts.

FAMILY EDUCATION

Duplicate and send home copies of "As a Family: Telling the Truth" (at the back of this guide).

LESSON 4
Worksheet

Name: _____

בִּרְכוֹת הַהַפְטָרָה

1. How many blessings are chanted *before* the haftarah reading? _____
   How many blessings are chanted *after* the haftarah reading? _____

2. Find the English meaning of the word הַפְטָרָה by unscrambling the following letters: ncoionscul. Write your answer on the line. _____

3. Write the English meaning on the line next to each Hebrew word below.

   תּוֹרָה _____   נְבִיאִים _____   כְּתוּבִים _____

4. Lightly circle the first letter in each Hebrew word in Question 3. Use the circled letters to help you answer the following:

   תַּנַ"ךְ is the name of the Hebrew Bible. How did the Hebrew Bible get its name?

   _____

   In which section of the תַּנַ"ךְ do we find the haftarah readings? _____

5. Write the number of each English word below next to its matching Hebrew root.

   1. compassion   2. holy   3. speak   4. bless, praise   5. choose   6. say

   אמר _____   דבר _____   בחר _____
   ברך _____   רחם _____   קדש _____

6. Write the number of each English word below next to the matching Hebrew word.

   1. righteousness, justice   2. truth   3. prophet   4. Israel
   5. Moses   6. God's people

   עַמּוֹ _____   צֶדֶק _____   אֱמֶת _____
   מֹשֶׁה _____   נָבִיא _____   יִשְׂרָאֵל _____

7. Name two qualities the prophets were required to have.

   _____

HINENI—THE NEW HEBREW THROUGH PRAYER 3 © Behrman House Publishers

LESSON 5

וְזֹאת הַתּוֹרָה\עֵץ חַיִּים הִיא\
עַל שְׁלֹשָׁה דְבָרִים

LEARNING OBJECTIVES

Prayer Reading Skills

- The prefixes וְ ("and"); הַ הָ ("the")
- The plural ending יִם (masc.)
- The roots דרכ ("road," "way"); עמד ("stand"); עבד ("worship" or "work");
- God's name, Adonai, is written יְיָ, יְהֹוָה

Prayer Concepts

- **וְזֹאת הַתּוֹרָה**

Moses taught the word of God to the Jewish people.

We lift the Torah scroll so the entire congregation can see the words of the Torah. *Hagbahah* is the term used for lifting the Torah scroll. The person lifting the scroll is called *magbiah* (masc.) or *magbihah* (fem.).

G'lilah is the term used for rolling and dressing the Torah scroll. The person rolling and dressing the scroll is called a *golel* (masc.) or *golelet* (fem.).

- **עֵץ חַיִּים הִיא**

The Torah is called עֵץ חַיִּים, a "tree of life." The Torah sustains the Jewish people.

The term עֲצֵי חַיִּים refers to the two wooden rollers that hold the parchment of the Torah scroll.

- **עַל שְׁלֹשָׁה דְבָרִים**

The world of Judaism stands on three things: Torah, worship, acts of loving-kindness—
תּוֹרָה, עֲבוֹדָה, גְּמִילוּת חֲסָדִים.

BEYOND THE TEXTBOOK

Reading Rules:

- The double-duty dot (מֹשֶׁה)
- The letter *vav* with a *dagesh* (וּ)
- The "eye" ending, אַי; the "ahv" ending, אָיו
- The double *sh'va* (ְּ)
- Double letters with *sh'va* (לְלוּ)

The root חסד ("kindness")

Citations: Book, Chapter, Verse (example: Numbers 9:23)

Holiday Connection: Shavuot; Simhat Torah

ABOUT THE PRAYER

When we complete the Torah reading, we hold up the Torah to show its words to the entire congregation. Traditionally, we believe that it was Moses who first taught the words of Torah to our people. When we return the Torah to the Ark, we do so with ceremony, just as we removed it with ceremony. This includes lifting our voices in song.

INSTRUCTIONAL MATERIALS

Text pages 46–59

Word Cards 39–59

Worksheet 5

Family Education: "As a Family: Roots and Branches" (at the back of this guide)

SET INDUCTION

The first of the three prayers in this chapter begins, "And this is the Torah that Moses placed before the people of Israel…."

You Are There

Ask the students to try to imagine themselves at the foot of Mount Sinai. Read the following paragraph to the class:

Moses has climbed to the top of the mountain. He remains there for forty days and forty nights. Through Moses, God makes a covenant with the people of Israel. The people of Israel are in the desert standing at the foot of the mountain. Moses is about to descend after his encounter with God. Imagine…

What does Moses' face look like?

How does his voice sound?

How deep is the hush of the people?

What are the people feeling?

Now read to the students the description in Exodus 34:27–33 of these events.

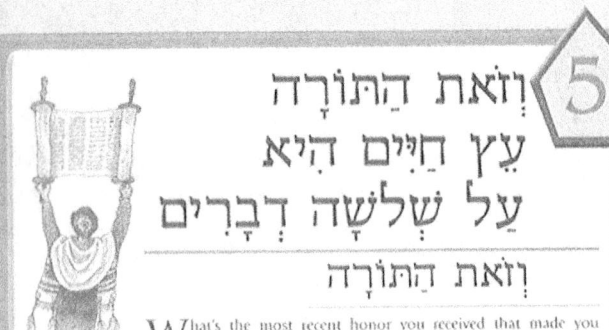

INTO THE TEXT

Call on students to read the three names at the top of the page.

וְזֹאת הַתּוֹרָה
עֵץ חַיִּים הִיא
עַל שְׁלֹשָׁה דְבָרִים

Choose students to read the introductory paragraph at the top of the page.

Ask students to share occasions on which they received an honor. How did they respond to the honor?

Explain that when the Torah is held up high for all to see (*hagbahah*), the person lifting the Torah turns his or her back to the congregation. In this way the words of Torah face the people.

Reading Rule Review: Double-Duty Dot

The dot in the name מֹשֶׁה (מֹש) serves two purposes.

- The dot is the "oh" vowel in מֹ.
- The dot indicates that the next letter is a *shin* (שׁ).

מֹ + שֶׁה = מֹשֶׁה

Reading Practice

Write the following words on the chalkboard for reading practice. Have students circle the double-duty dot in each word. Ask students to read each word aloud.

חֹשֶׁךְ   קֹדֶשׁ   שְׁלֹשָׁה   מֹשֶׁה

Which of the four words is found in the name of a prayer at the top of the page? (שְׁלֹשָׁה)

Have students lightly circle the name מֹשֶׁה in lines 1 and 2.

Ask: What is the English name for מֹשֶׁה? (*Moses*)

Call on students to read the prayer, first in unison and then individually.

Read the English meaning of the prayer aloud.

PRAYER DICTIONARY

Display Word Cards 39–44 in random order.

Call on the students to read:

- the three words with a שׁ or a שׂ.
  (שָׁם מֹשֶׁה יִשְׂרָאֵל)
- the two words that rhyme. (לִפְנֵי בְּנֵי)

Ask students to try to give the English meaning of as many of the Word Cards as possible. Have them read the remaining words and the English meaning on the back of each card.

Challenge the students to read each Hebrew word and give the English meaning without looking at the back of the Word Card.

SEARCH AND CIRCLE

Have students cover the Prayer Dictionary and complete the activity.

Assign one row of words to five different students. Each student should read aloud the English as well as the three Hebrew words or phrases in the assigned row. The class should respond in unison with the correct Hebrew word match.

Photo Op

Read the caption aloud to the students.

Review the meaning behind this ritual by having students silently read the last sentence in the second paragraph on page 46. Ask the students to explain it in their own words.

WHAT'S MISSING?

Direct students to complete the exercise individually. They can use the Word Cards and the prayer on page 46 to assist them in spelling the Hebrew words correctly.

Challenge: What is the English meaning of each missing word? (*the Torah, Moses, Israel, Moses*)

Have students read the completed sentence in unison and individually.

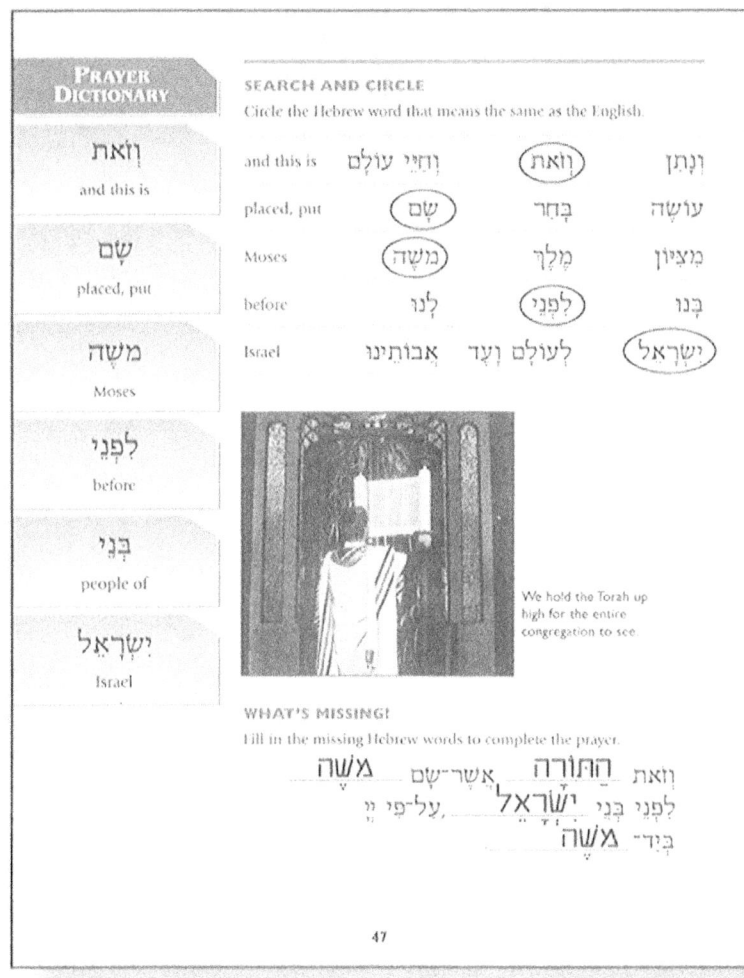

65   LESSON 5

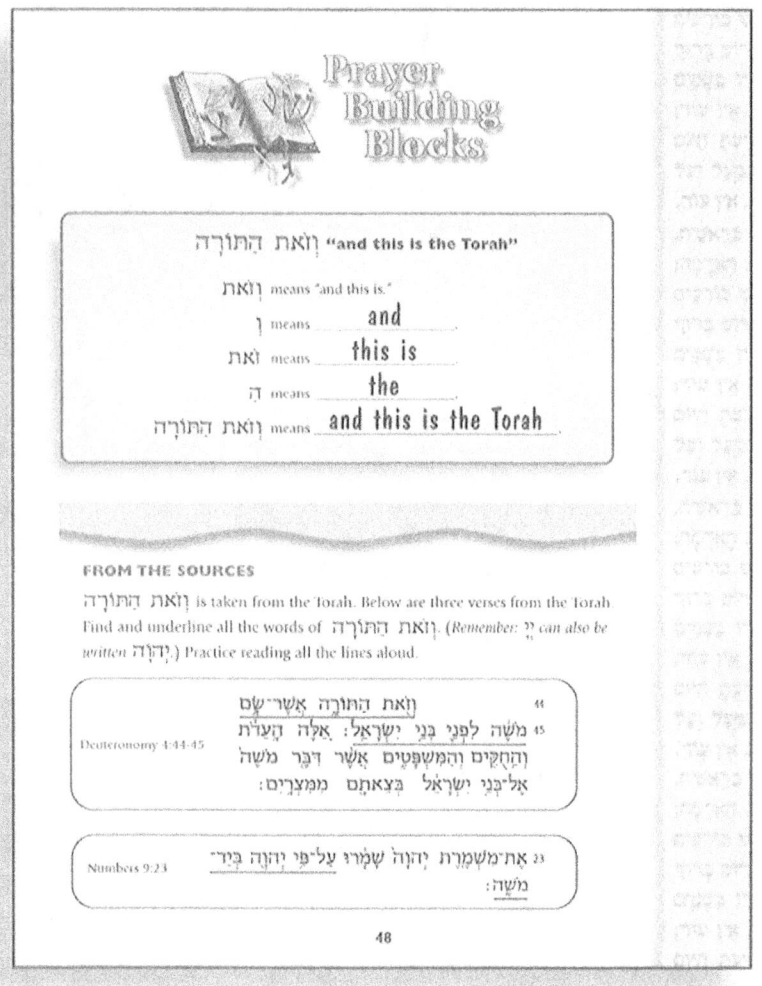

PRAYER BUILDING BLOCKS

וְזֹאת הַתּוֹרָה
"and this is the Torah"

Review the prefixes וְ ("and") and הַ ("the") with the students.

Complete the exercise together.

FROM THE SOURCES

After students have completed the activity, call on individuals to read the underlined selections aloud.

Write the names of the Five Books of Moses on the chalkboard in right-to-left order.

בְּרֵאשִׁית שְׁמוֹת וַיִּקְרָא בְּמִדְבַּר דְּבָרִים

Deuteronomy Numbers Leviticus Exodus Genesis

Explain that each book is divided into chapters and verses. A verse is like a sentence.

The books are divided into chapters and verses only in the printed form of the Torah, *not* in the *sefer Torah*—the Torah scroll—itself.

Write the citations on the chalkboard for the selections given.

    Deuteronomy 4:44–45   Numbers 9:23

Explain that the chapters and verses are numbered. The chapter number appears before the colon (9:) The verse number(s) appear after the colon (:23). Ask the students to read each citation. (*Book of Deuteronomy, Chapter 4, Verses 44 through 45; Book of Numbers, Chapter 9, Verse 23*)

Direct students to the Torah selections in From the Sources.

- Have the students circle both citations. (*Deuteronomy 4:44–45; Numbers 9:23*)
- Ask: In the first citation, what are the verse numbers? (*44, 45*)
- Explain that a double diamond indicates the conclusion of a verse.

    What word concludes verse 44? (יִשְׂרָאֵל) begins verse 45? (אֵלֶּה)

- Ask students to name the book, chapter, and verse for the underlined *opening* words of וְזֹאת הַתּוֹרָה. (*Book of Deuteronomy, Chapter 4, Verse 44*)
- Ask students to name the book, chapter, and verse for the underlined *concluding* words of the prayer. (*Book of Numbers, Chapter 9, Verse 23*)

THE NEW HEBREW THROUGH PRAYER 3 • הִנְנִי   66

אֲשֶׁר־שָׂם מֹשֶׁה
"that Moses placed"

Complete the Building Block together.

Call on individual students to read each of the four lines in the Building Block exercise.

Have students read the following words as well as the phrases that contains the words.

- The word in line 2 that means "prophet." (נָבִיא)
- The line from the blessing before the haftarah reading. (*line 3*)
- The word in line 4 that has the letter *vav* with a *dagesh*. (צִוָּה) Write צִוָּה on the chalkboard. Ask students to explain why ו in the word צִוָּה is the letter *vav* with a *dagesh* and not the vowel "oo." (*the letter before the ו already has a vowel; the ו has a vowel of its own*)

לִפְנֵי בְּנֵי יִשְׂרָאֵל
"before the people of Israel"

Have students complete the exercise individually and share their answers with the class.

Read the complete prayer aloud.

A Musical Note

Teach the students to chant the prayer with the melody used in your synagogue.

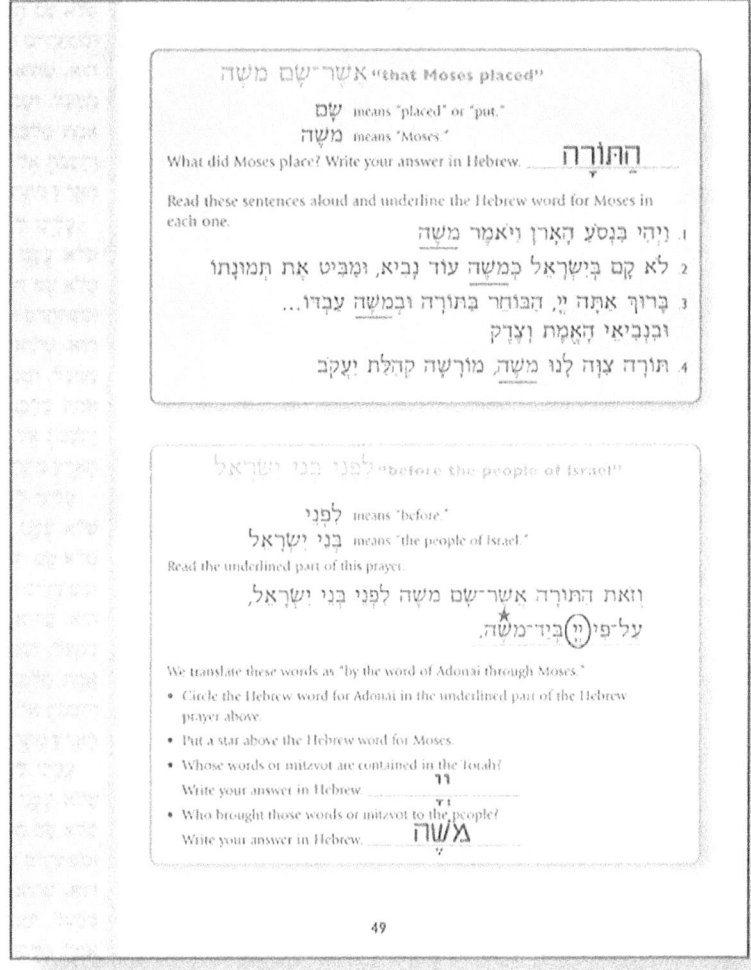

Holiday Connection

Shavuot ("weeks") celebrates the giving of the Torah to the people of Israel seven weeks

after the Exodus from Egypt. Our tradition teaches us that God gave the Torah to the

people of Israel through Moses (בְּיַד־מֹשֶׁה).

Ask the students to circle this phrase in the prayer on page 46.

INTRODUCING
עֵץ חַיִּים הִיא

Ask the students to describe the qualities of a tree. (*represents life and growth; is strong; has deep roots; has branches; can be a source of food; provides beauty, shade, and protection*)

Explain that the Torah is known as a "tree of life"—עֵץ חַיִּים.

Ask: Why is the metaphor of the Torah as a tree of life an appropriate one? (*the Torah gives life to the Jewish people; it has roots in our past and branches throughout the generations; it is a source of nourishment for the soul of the people; it is beautifully dressed*)

Into the Prayer

Call on students to read aloud the introduction to the lesson at the top of the page.

Direct students to highlight or underline key words and phrases in the introductory paragraph that liken the Torah to a tree. (*living thing; roots and branches; grow; flourish; live*)

Call on a student to read the English translation of the prayer aloud. Then choose one or more students to read the prayer in Hebrew.

As a Family

You may wish to send home copies of the "As a Family: Roots and Branches" page at this time.

Reading Practice

Call on students to read aloud each word that has:

- a *dagesh* that does not change the sound of the letter in which it is found.
- a final letter.
- the letter-vowel combination הָ at the end of the word.
- the sound-alike letters ח or כ.

Select four students and have each read one phrase in turn. Repeat several times with different groups of four students.

Read the complete prayer in unison with the students.

PRAYER DICTIONARY

Call on seven students to stand in random order and display Word Cards 45–51 to the rest of the class.

Direct the students holding the following words to step forward and display their cards in the correct Hebrew order of the prayer:

- the phrase meaning "its ways are ways of pleasantness" (48, 49, 50)
- the word meaning "peace" (51)
- the phrase meaning "tree of life" (45, 46)
- the words meaning "happy" (47) and "pleasantness" (50)

Have the students complete the Match Game and Descriptive Words activities to review and reinforce vocabulary.

Photo Op

Call on a student to read the caption aloud.

Holiday Connection:

Ask students for the name of the holiday that celebrates the completion of the yearly Torah reading cycle and the start of the new cycle. (*Simḥat Torah—Rejoicing of the Torah*) Why do we immediately start reading the Torah from the beginning? (*to indicate our devotion to the study of Torah; to symbolize the continual cycle of Torah reading and Torah study; as a continuous reminder of our history, our laws, and our relationship with God*)

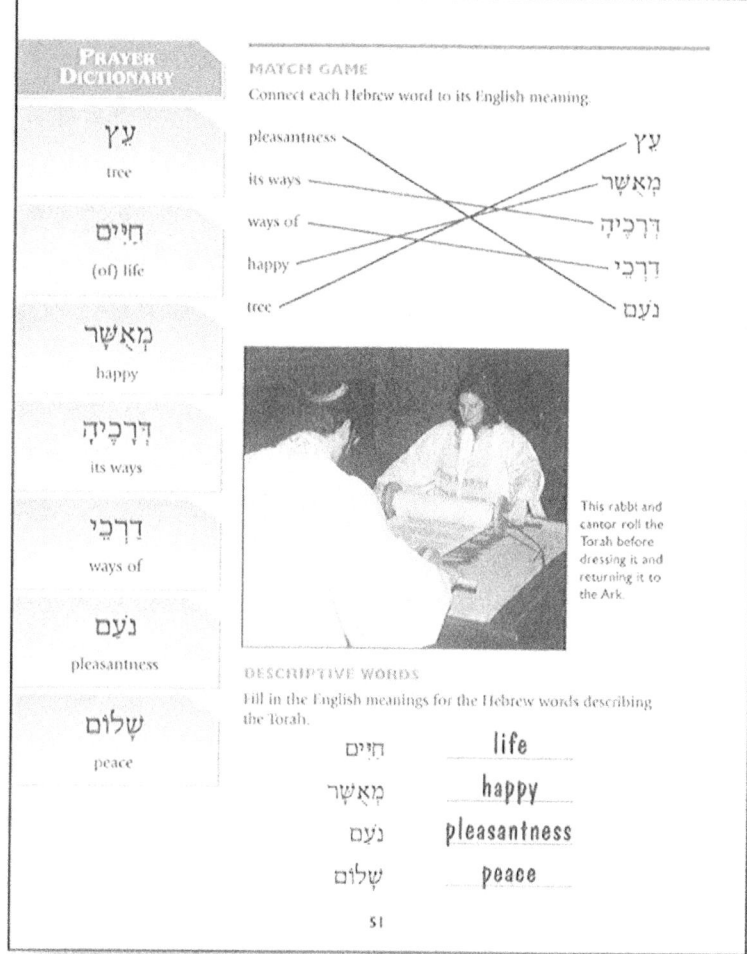

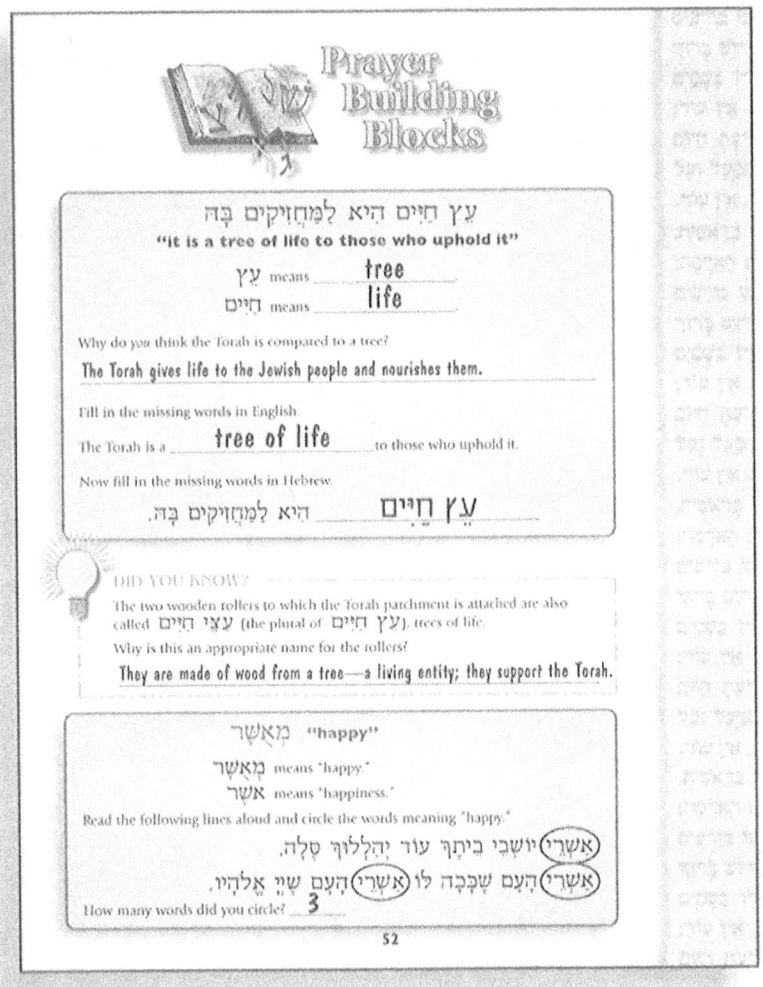

Have each student read one word in turn in lines 1–2. Continue repeating the lines until all the students have had the opportunity to read.

Read the selection in unison with the students. Call on individual students to read each line.

The first three words mean "Happy are they who dwell in Your house." Ask:

- Who are "they"? (*the Jewish people*)
- Whose "house" does the prayer refer to? (*God's house*)
- How would you interpret the phrase "God's house"? (*the Holy Temple; the synagogue*)

PRAYER BUILDING BLOCKS

עֵץ חַיִּים הִיא לַמַּחֲזִיקִים בָּהּ

"it is a tree of life to those who uphold it"

Have students complete the Building Block.

Encourage them to draw upon class discussions to explain why the Torah is compared to a tree.

Review all the answers.

DID YOU KNOW?

Read the statement aloud.

Brainstorm answers to the question. Write the ideas on the chalkboard. Have the students write their responses on the line provided.

מְאַשֵּׁר "happy"

The two Hebrew sentences are the opening lines in the Ashrei prayer, chanted in many synagogues during the Torah service.

Call on students to read each word:

- meaning "happy." (אַשְׁרֵי)
- with a letter that changes its form at the end of the word (a final letter). (בֵיתֶךָ יְהַלְלוּךָ הָעָם)
- with a *dagesh* that does or does not change the sound of the letter in which it is found. (סֶלָה שֶׁכָּכָה לוֹ)
- with God's name. (שֶׁיְיָ אֱלֹהָיו)

THE NEW HEBREW THROUGH PRAYER 3 • הִנְנִי

דְּרָכֶיהָ דַרְכֵי נֹעַם
"its ways are ways of pleasantness"

Read the Building Block aloud with the students.

Write the phrase דֶּרֶךְ אֶרֶץ on the chalkboard. Tell students that the phrase, refers to the mitzvah of good manners—the right way to behave.

The Fruit of the Tree

Create fruit using the words from the Building Block phrase, and place on the דרכ tree.

Reading Skills

Review the following reading skills, and then call on students to read lines 1 and 2.

- Write יְ, ְי, ָי on the chalkboard. Ask the students to read each sound. Reminder: ַי ("eye") and ָיו ("ahv") only appear at the *end* of a word. Call on students to read the fourth and last words on line 1.

- Write a double *sh'va* on the chalkboard (ְ ְ). Remind students that the first *sh'va* is silent. The second *sh'va* is sounded. Call on students to read the words in line 2 with a double *sh'va* (בְּשִׁבְתְּךָ, וּבְלֶכְתְּךָ, וּבְשָׁכְבְּךָ).

- **Prayer Challenge:** Ask which line comes from the V'ahavta. (*line 2*)

FROM THE SOURCES

- Review: Ask the students to name the three sections in the תָּנָ"ךְ. (תּוֹרָה, נְבִיאִים, כְּתוּבִים) (*Torah, Prophets, Writings*)

- Call on a student to write the following citation on the chalkboard in the format used to indicate biblical chapters and verses: "Proverbs, Chapter 3, Verses 16 through 18." (*Proverbs 3:16–18*)

- Explain that Proverbs, an ancient collection of wise sayings and short parables, is found in the third section of the תָּנָ"ךְ.

Read the introductory sentences of this activity aloud with the students.

Direct the students to read the prayer on page 50 to help them complete the exercise.

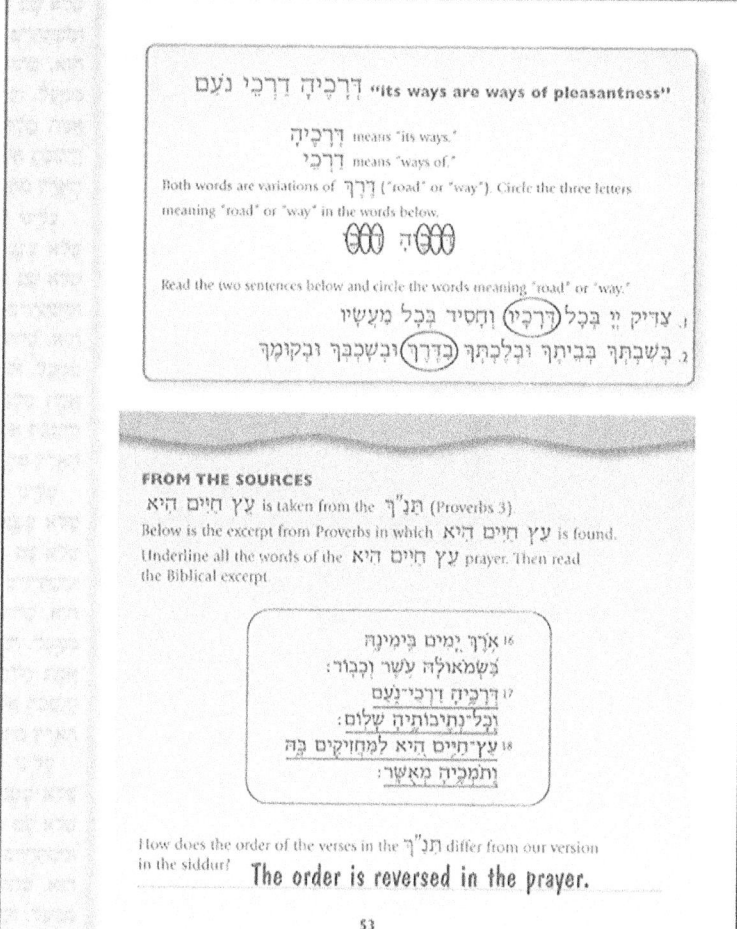

INTRODUCING
עַל שְׁלשָׁה דְבָרִים

Draw a large globe of the world on a sheet of paper or on the chalkboard.

Draw a "stand" for it with three legs.

Ask: What three things do you think we need

- for the world to stand strong so that we may live?
- for Judaism to stand strong so that the Jewish people may live?

Into the Prayer

Read aloud the introduction to the prayer.

Explain to students that *Al Sh'loshah D'varim* comes from Pirke Avot and has been incorporated, usually in Reform synagogues, into the Torah service.

Ask: What does the prayer tell us is needed to keep our people's souls, heritage, and strength alive? (*the teachings of the Torah, believing in and serving God, and acts of goodness toward others*)

Point out the equivalent Hebrew words:

תּוֹרָה	עֲבוֹדָה	גְמִילוּת חֲסָדִים
Torah	worship	acts of loving-kindness

Read the English translation of the prayer.

On the drawing of the globe of the world, write the three items on which the world stands, one item on each leg. Add the Hebrew term for each.

Reading Practice

Read lines 1–2 in unison.

Break-Away Reading:
Select three students. Have *all* the students read line 1 in unison, then complete the prayer in the following way:

Student A reads עַל הַתּוֹרָה ("on the Torah").

Student B reads וְעַל הָעֲבוֹדָה ("and on the worship").

Student C reads וְעַל גְמִילוּת חֲסָדִים ("and on acts of loving-kindness").

THE NEW HEBREW THROUGH PRAYER 3 • הִנְנִי   72

PRAYER DICTIONARY

Display Word Cards 57, 58, and 59 in random order on the edge of the chalkboard.

Ask half the class to read each Hebrew word. Ask the other half to give its English meaning. Assign one student to turn the cards for the class to check the answers.

Reinforcing Word Order

Chooose one or more of the Reinforcing Word Order games described at the front of this guide (page 7).

FILL IN THE BLANKS

Have students complete the exercise and review together.

Photo Op

Call on a student to read the caption aloud.

Assign students the task of searching the web for organizations that help those in need. Ask them to report back to the class on a designated date. For each organization found on the "mitzvah machine"—the computer—students should be prepared to give the following information: name of the organization(s), location, goals, how monies and time are allocated, success stories, and how the students might support the work of the organization. Choose an organization for the class to become involved in.

WHAT'S WRONG?

Read the directions with the students. Note that there can be more than one meaning for a word.

Have the students complete the exercise with a study partner. Call on partners to share their answers with the class.

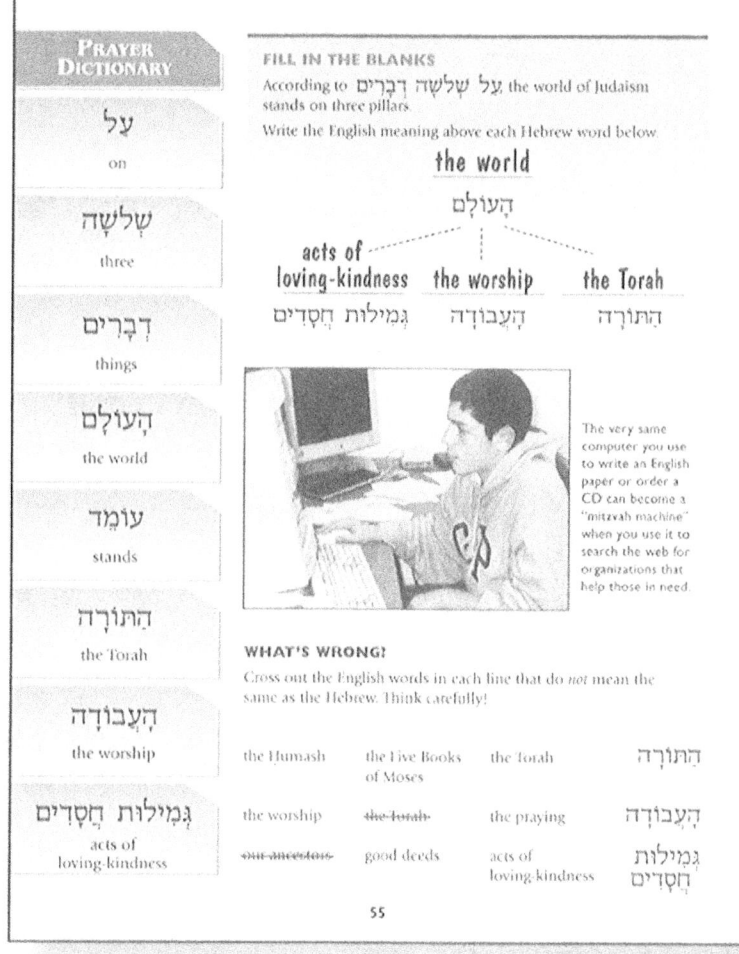

73   LESSON 5

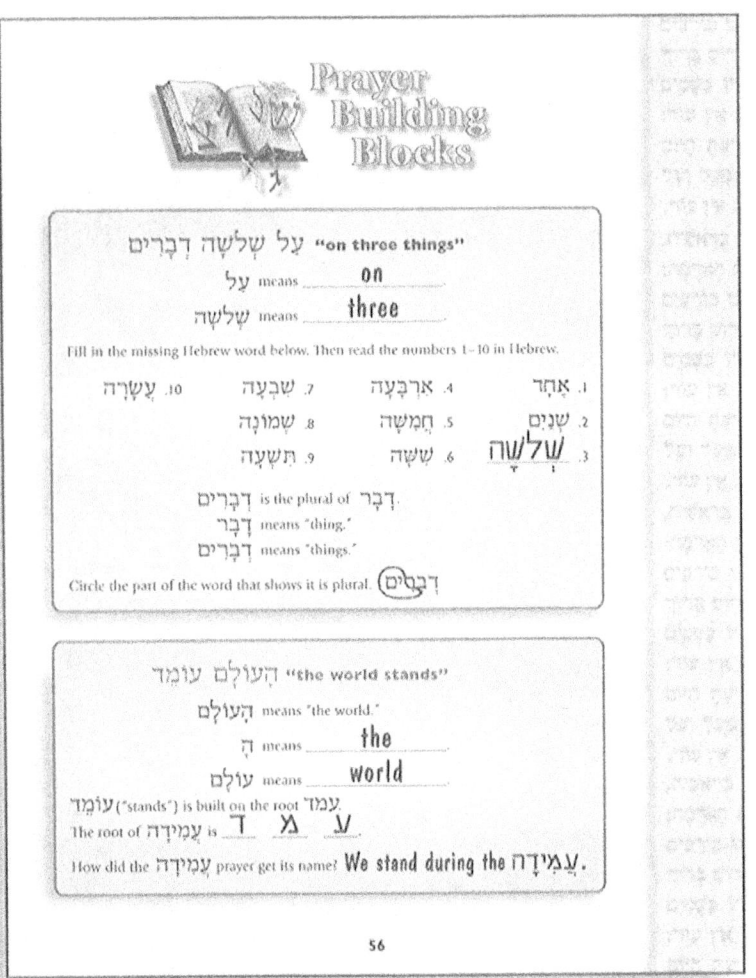

PRAYER BUILDING BLOCKS

עַל שְׁלֹשָׁה דְבָרִים "on three things"

Read and complete the Building Block with the students.

Count It Out

Have students count off 1–10, then read their Hebrew number in order. Have them count off again, starting with a different student, and repeat the activity.

Count on It!

Give each student ten index cards or pieces of paper, one for each of the ten numbers.

Students should write each numeral on one side of the card and the corresponding Hebrew word on the other side.

The students can use these personal flashcards to learn the Hebrew numbers.

הָעוֹלָם עוֹמֵד "the world stands"

Read the Building Block with the students.

Pass out Word Cards 52–56 to five students. The students should stand up, one at a time, in the correct order and read aloud their word. Repeat using the English side of the Word Cards.

Call on students to read page 54, line 1.

The Fruit of the Tree

Create a fruit tree with the root עמד. Write "stand" on the trunk of the tree.

Use words from the Building Block to make fruit for the tree.

עַל הַתּוֹרָה "on the Torah"

Read the explanation aloud to the students.

Discuss their responses to the question.

Practice reciting the blessing we say before we study Torah.

The English meaning of the blessing is "Praised are You, Adonai our God, Ruler of the universe, who has made us holy through mitzvot and commands us to engage in the study of Torah."

Ask: Why do we recite a blessing praising God for the mitzvah of Torah study? (*to remind ourselves we are about to perform a holy act; to show we recognize our obligation to study Torah*)

Note: The blessing has become part of the morning service—it is not recited before Torah study by those who have already said it once in the morning.

הָעֲבוֹדָה "the worship"

Have students complete the Building Block.

עַל הַתּוֹרָה "on the Torah"

We know that הַתּוֹרָה means "the Torah."
But הַתּוֹרָה is not just the scroll we read.
הַתּוֹרָה means studying the writings of the Torah and learning from it how to worship God (הָעֲבוֹדָה) and how to be a good person (גְמִילוּת חֲסָדִים).
How can studying the Torah teach us how to act toward God and toward other people?

The mitzvot in the Torah teach us how to act. We learn about decisions our ancestors made in their relationship with God and people.

Read the בְּרָכָה that we say before studying the Torah.

בָּרוּךְ אַתָּה, יְיָ אֱלֹהֵינוּ, מֶלֶךְ הָעוֹלָם,
אֲשֶׁר קִדְּשָׁנוּ בְּמִצְוֹתָיו וְצִוָּנוּ לַעֲסֹק בְּדִבְרֵי תוֹרָה.

הָעֲבוֹדָה "the worship"

הָעֲבוֹדָה is made up of two parts
הָ means **the**
עֲבוֹדָה means "worship" or "service to God."
הָעֲבוֹדָה means **the worship**

The root of עֲבוֹדָה is עבד.
When a word has the root עבד, this tells us that "worship" or "work" is part of its meaning.

57

---

75 LESSON 5

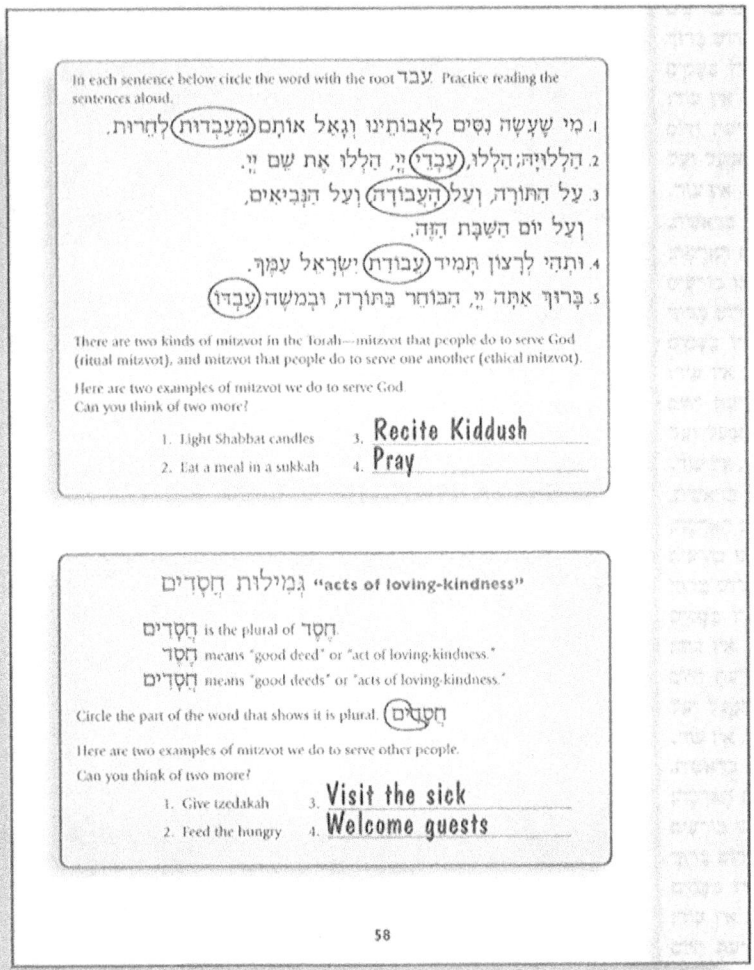

עָבַד

Direct students to complete the activity.

Call on students to read the circled words aloud.

Reading Rule: When the same letter appears consecutively in a word (לל) and the first one has a sh'va (לְלוּ), the sh'va is sounded.

Have students draw a box around the letters לְלוּ in line 2. Call on students to read each word with a box. (הַ לְלוּ יָהּ   הַ לְלוּ   הַ לְלוּ)

Call on individual students to read each line aloud.

Prayer Challenge: Which two lines are part of the haftarah blessings? (lines 3 and 5)

Ask students to answer the question, then share their responses with the class.

The Fruit of the Tree

Create a fruit tree with the root עָבַד. Write "worship" and "work" on the trunk. Add fruit with the words from the Building Block as well as the circled words in lines 1–5.

גְּמִילוּת חֲסָדִים
"acts of loving-kindness"

Read the Building Block aloud with the students.

Ask: What is the root of the words חֶסֶד and חֲסָדִים? (חסד, "kindness")

Have students answer the question, then share their responses with the class.

Call on each student to read page 54, lines 1–2.

The Fruit of the Tree

Create a fruit tree with the root חסד. Add fruit with the word from the Building Block phrase to the tree.

A Musical Note

Teach the students the melody for the prayer.

Is this prayer part of the Torah service in your synagogue?

An Enriching Experience

Develop a class mitzvah project that reflects the concept of גְּמִילוּת חֲסָדִים.
(*Examples: holding a toy, clothing, or food drive; sending birthday cards to senior citizens in your synagogue or a local nursing home; inviting senior citizens to a class Shabbat dinner; collecting toiletries for a shelter*)

End Games

Play one of the games described in the Classroom Games at the front of this guide (pages 9–11) to review concepts and vocabulary for the three prayers in Chapter 5.

A Model Torah Service

Review the prayers and rituals taught in Chapters 1–5.

Plan a model service in the sanctuary. You may wish to invite your students' families to join you.

FLUENT READING

Have the class form two groups by counting off 1–2, 1–2, and so on.

All the 1s should form a group. All the 2s should form another group.

The 1s should meet and practice reading the odd-numbered lines: 1, 3, 5, 7.

The 2s should meet and practice the even-numbered lines: 2, 4, 6.

Group members can assist each other with reading skills.

Call on each group to read the assigned lines in unison, then individually.

WORKSHEET

Duplicate and hand out copies of the worksheet for Lesson 5 to review skills and concepts.

FAMILY EDUCATION

Duplicate and send home copies of "As a Family: Roots and Branches" (at the back of this guide) if you did not already do so.

FLUENT READING

Each line below contains a word you know. Practice reading the lines.

1. תְּהִלַּת יְיָ יְדַבֶּר פִּי, וִיבָרֵךְ כָּל בָּשָׂר שֵׁם קָדְשׁוֹ לְעוֹלָם וָעֶד.

2. וּדְבַר אֶחָד מִדְּבָרֶיךָ אָחוֹר לֹא יָשׁוּב רֵיקָם.

3. בֵּינִי וּבֵין בְּנֵי יִשְׂרָאֵל אוֹת הִיא לְעֹלָם.

4. שֶׁלֹּא עָשָׂנוּ כְּגוֹיֵי הָאֲרָצוֹת וְלֹא שָׂמָנוּ כְּמִשְׁפְּחוֹת הָאֲדָמָה.

5. שְׁלֹשָׁה מִי יוֹדֵעַ? שְׁלֹשָׁה אֲנִי יוֹדֵעַ. שְׁלֹשָׁה אָבוֹת, שְׁנֵי לֻחוֹת הַבְּרִית, אֶחָד אֱלֹהֵינוּ שֶׁבַּשָּׁמַיִם וּבָאָרֶץ.

6. וּלְקַיֵּם אֶת כָּל דִּבְרֵי תַלְמוּד תּוֹרָתֶךָ בְּאַהֲבָה.

7. בָּרוּךְ אַתָּה, יְיָ, גּוֹמֵל חֲסָדִים טוֹבִים לְעַמּוֹ יִשְׂרָאֵל.

LESSON 5
Worksheet

Name: _____

וְזֹאת הַתּוֹרָה \ עֵץ חַיִּים הִיא \ עַל שְׁלֹשָׁה דְּבָרִים

1. Number the English and Hebrew phrases in the correct order of וְזֹאת הַתּוֹרָה.

   ____ through Moses   ____ אֲשֶׁר־שָׂם מֹשֶׁה

   ____ and this is the Torah   ____ עַל־פִּי יְיָ

   ____ before the people of Israel   ____ וְזֹאת הַתּוֹרָה

   ____ by the word of Adonai   ____ בְּיַד־מֹשֶׁה

   ____ that Moses placed   ____ לִפְנֵי בְּנֵי יִשְׂרָאֵל

   Write the Hebrew word for "Moses." _____

   Write the Hebrew word for "Israel." _____

2. Explain each Torah term below.

   hagbahah _____

   g'lilah _____

3. What is the meaning of the phrase עֵץ חַיִּים? _____

   Explain in your own words why the Torah is called עֵץ חַיִּים.

   _____

   _____

4. Using the following Hebrew words, fill in the missing words and phrases in the prayer below.

   הָעֲבוֹדָה   גְּמִילוּת חֲסָדִים   הַתּוֹרָה

   עַל שְׁלֹשָׁה דְבָרִים הָעוֹלָם עוֹמֵד:

   The world stands on three things:

   עַל _____ וְעַל _____ וְעַל _____

   on Torah   on worship   and on acts of loving-kindness

5. Explain each of the following terms and give an example.

   Torah: _____

   worship: _____

   acts of loving-kindness: _____

HINENI—THE NEW HEBREW THROUGH PRAYER 3 © Behrman House Publishers

LESSON 6 עָלֵינוּ

LEARNING OBJECTIVES

Prayer Reading Skills
- The prefix וֹ ("and")
- The suffix נוּ ("us" or "our")
- The root מלכ ("rule")

Prayer Concepts
- Aleinu expresses our loyalty to God.
- We bend our knees and bow when we recite Aleinu. In this way, we act out the words of the prayer and show respect and honor for God.
- Aleinu symbolizes the sacrifice of Jewish men and women who refused to convert to other religions.
- Aleinu was first chanted in the Rosh Hashanah service before it became part of the daily prayer service.
- Ethical Echo: בְּצֶלֶם אֱלֹהִים ("in the image of God")

BEYOND THE TEXTBOOK
Reading Rule: "ah" (הָ) ending

ABOUT THE PRAYER
In Aleinu, we acknowledge God as the Creator and Ruler of the universe. We "bend the knee, bow, and give thanks" before God in recognition and acceptance of God's rule. We accept the role God has assigned to us and we pray for a world of peace and unity among all people.

INSTRUCTIONAL MATERIALS
Text pages 60–67

Word Cards 60–69

Worksheet 6

Family Education: "As a Family: Showing Respect for God" (at the back of this guide)

SET INDUCTION
Explain to the class that Aleinu talks of our hope for a perfect world, one in which people are united under God's rule.

Ask: How can we work toward that goal? What unites people? What divides them?

Develop the following visualization to help students answer these questions.

Visualizing Answers
Draw a large globe (circle) on the chalkboard or on a sheet of paper.

Inside the globe, draw a pattern of zigzag lines symbolizing a divided and broken world in need of repair. Label the globe "A Broken World."

Draw a second globe on the chalkboard or on paper, and let it remain whole. Label it "A United World."

Ask the students to think about actions, ideas, or emotions that divide people. (*arguments, anger, friction, hurt, war, insults, bias*) Write their suggestions inside the broken globe.

Ask the students to think about actions, ideas, or emotions that unite people. (*friendship, sharing, help, kindness, love, care, common goals, tolerance*) Write their suggestions inside the whole globe.

INTO THE TEXT

Read the introduction to the lesson with the students.

Ask them in what ways they have pledged their loyalty. (*American Pledge of Allegiance; reciting the Sh'ma; boy or girl scout oath*)

Ask individual students to recite a pledge. Discuss its intent. (*Pledge of Allegiance: loyalty to our country and the right of liberty and justice for those living here; Sh'ma: allegiance to One God; scout's oath: loyalty to God and country*)

Call on students to read the English translation of the prayer aloud.

Reading Practice

Reading Rule: When ה comes at the end of a word, the vowel ַ is read first ("ah").

Write the following words on the chalkboard: רוּחַ כֹּחַ מָשִׁיחַ לְשַׁבֵּחַ

Call on one student to read the first part of each word aloud. Have the class read the ending ה sound. For example: student, רוּ; class, חַ.

Ask the students to match one of the words on the chalkboard with a word in line 1 of the prayer. (לְשַׁבֵּחַ)

Have the students count off 1, 2, 3 around the room to form groups of three students each. Groups should meet and practice reading the prayer. Each group member should read two words in turn.

There are three Hebrew sentences in the prayer excerpt and corresponding English sentences. Divide the class in two. Have one half of the class read the Hebrew sentences. The second half should read the corresponding English. Then switch so the second half now reads the Hebrew and the first half reads the English.

PRAYER DICTIONARY

Display Word Cards 60–69. Call on students to read each word or phrase.

Read the English meaning on the back of each Word Card.

The Word Cards reflect key themes in the prayer. As the students work through the Prayer Building Blocks, the Word Cards can be utilized to highlight the concepts and enhance reading skills.

FREE CHOICE

Display the Word Cards on the edge of the chalkboard.

Allow students several minutes to complete the exercise. Call on students to share their choices with the class.

Photo Op

Call on a student to read the caption. Explain that the *huppah*—wedding canopy—represents the couple's new home. Under the *huppah*, the bride and groom are made holy to one another, just as the Jewish people were made holy to God at Mount Sinai when they promised they would worship only God.

PRAYER BACKGROUND

Write questions on the chalkboard about the paragraph. (See sample questions below.)

Direct the students to read the paragraph silently and to underline the answers to the questions you have written.

Sample Questions: How old is Aleinu? During what service was the prayer originally chanted? When did it become part of the daily prayer service? What is the theme of Aleinu?

Call on students to share their answers aloud.

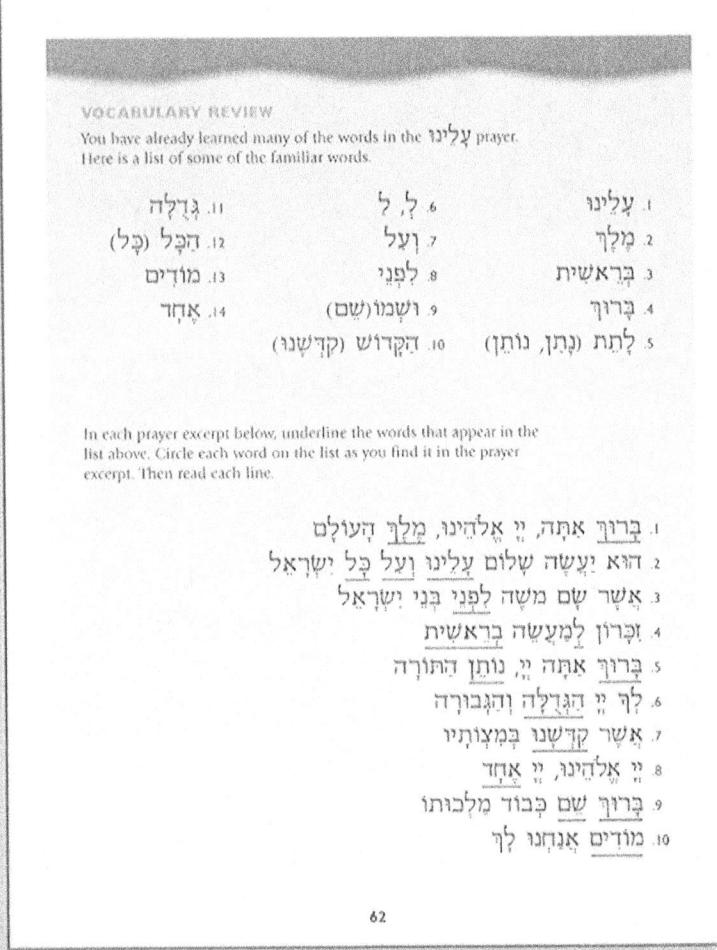

VOCABULARY REVIEW

Call on students to read aloud words on the list. Have students follow the directions in the middle of the page. Call on individuals to read the circled words aloud and then read the complete line that contains each word.

Word Know-How

Ask students to find the words described below in the ten prayer lines on the page. The numbers below correspond to the line numbers. After reading the word or phrase, have students read the complete line aloud.

Find and read the word(s) or phrase(s):

1. built on the root "bless" (בָּרוּךְ); meaning "ruler." (מֶלֶךְ)
2. meaning "peace" (שָׁלוֹם); meaning "Israel" (יִשְׂרָאֵל); built on the root "do" or "make." (יַעֲשֶׂה)
3. with a double-duty dot. (מֹשֶׁה)
4. meaning "creation" (בְּרֵאשִׁית); built on the root meaning "do" or "make." (לְמַעֲשֵׂה)
5. meaning "who gives us the Torah." (נוֹתֵן הַתּוֹרָה)
6. with the prefix meaning "the" (הַגְּדֻלָּה, וְהַגְּבוּרָה); with two prefixes meaning "and the." (וְהַגְּבוּרָה)
7. built on the root "holy." (קִדְּשָׁנוּ)
8. meaning "God is One." (יְיָ אֶחָד)
9. built on the root "rule." (מַלְכוּתוֹ)
10. meaning "thank." (מוֹדִים)

Challenge

Ask students to identify the prayers or blessings from which these lines are taken.
(1. blessing "formula"; 2. Oseh Shalom; 3. V'zot Hatorah; 4. Kiddush; 5. Torah blessings; 6. L'cha Adonai; 7. blessing of mitzvah; 8. Sh'ma; 9. Sh'ma second line; 10. blessing in the Amidah—Hoda'ah)

PRAYER BUILDING BLOCKS

עָלֵינוּ לְשַׁבֵּחַ לַאֲדוֹן הַכֹּל
"it is our duty to praise the God of all"

Call on students to read the Building Block phrase aloud.

Give four students Word Cards 60–63 in random order.

Have the students stand facing the class with their words in the order of the Building Block phrase. Have each say the word aloud.

Repeat the activity with the English side of the cards.

Read the Building Block activity aloud with the students.

Ask if they recognize the prayer excerpt. (*Oseh Shalom*)

וַאֲנַחְנוּ כּוֹרְעִים וּמִשְׁתַּחֲוִים וּמוֹדִים
"and we bend the knee and bow and thank God"

Display Word Cards 64 and 65.

Call on students to read aloud the Hebrew words and give their English meanings.

Choose a student to read the Building Block phrase.

Ask which word(s) or phrase(s) in the Building Block

- mean "and we" (וַאֲנַחְנוּ); "and thank." (וּמוֹדִים)
- means "bend the knee and bow." (כּוֹרְעִים וּמִשְׁתַּחֲוִים)
- have the prefix meaning "and." (וַאֲנַחְנוּ, וּמִשְׁתַּחֲוִים, וּמוֹדִים)

83   LESSON 6

HOW TO BOW

Read and complete this section with the students.

Have students turn to page 60. Recite lines 1 and 2 together.

Ask the students to stand and to read the first four words in line 2, to bend their knees (כּוֹרְעִים), and to bow (וּמִשְׁתַּחֲוִים).

As a Family

You might wish to send home a copy of "As a Family: Showing Respect for God" with each student at this time.

לִפְנֵי מֶלֶךְ מַלְכֵי הַמְּלָכִים
"before the Ruler of rulers"

Call on students to read the Building Block phrase.

Complete the Building Block with the students.

Tongue Twister

See how quickly students can say the Building Block phrase without twisting their tongues.

Photo Op

Call on a student to read the caption and the boy's sign in the photo.

Ask: What does "solidarity" mean? (*loyalty, common interests*)

Why do Jewish people throughout the world demonstrate solidarity with Israel? (*Israel is the homeland of the Jewish people; it is the land God promised us [Genesis 12:1–7; 13:14–17]*)

בַּיּוֹם הַהוּא יְהְיֶה יְיָ אֶחָד וּשְׁמוֹ אֶחָד

"on that day, Adonai will be one and God's name will be one"

Call on students to read the Building Block phrase aloud.

Direct the students to the days of the week in the activity.

Point out that the Hebrew translations for the days of the week are not names, like Monday and Tuesday, but numbers (first day, second day). The exception is Shabbat, the seventh day.

Ask: Why do you think we call the seventh day by a name and not a number? (*the seventh day was blessed by God after the work of creation [Genesis 2:1–3]*)

Call on students to recite the Hebrew names of the days of the week.

Challenge them to recite the days of the week from memory.

A Daily Chart

Have each student draw and then cut out a large circle from poster board, and divide it into seven segments. Students should label the segments with the Hebrew name for each day of the week, allowing space for illustrations reflecting their activities on each day.

Examples: יוֹם רִאשׁוֹן—baseball practice; יוֹם שַׁבָּת—religious school; יוֹם שְׁלִישִׁי—family dinner or cousin's Bat Mitzvah.

PRAYING TOGETHER

Ask students what they think the advantage is of praying together in a community. (*provides a sense of belonging and commonality; people can support each other in sad times; can celebrate with each other in happy times*)

Note: A *minyan* is not required for the recitation of Aleinu.

Read the introductory explanation aloud and have students complete the activity. Ask them to combine the ideas in the paragraph with their own ideas to respond to the question at the bottom of the page.

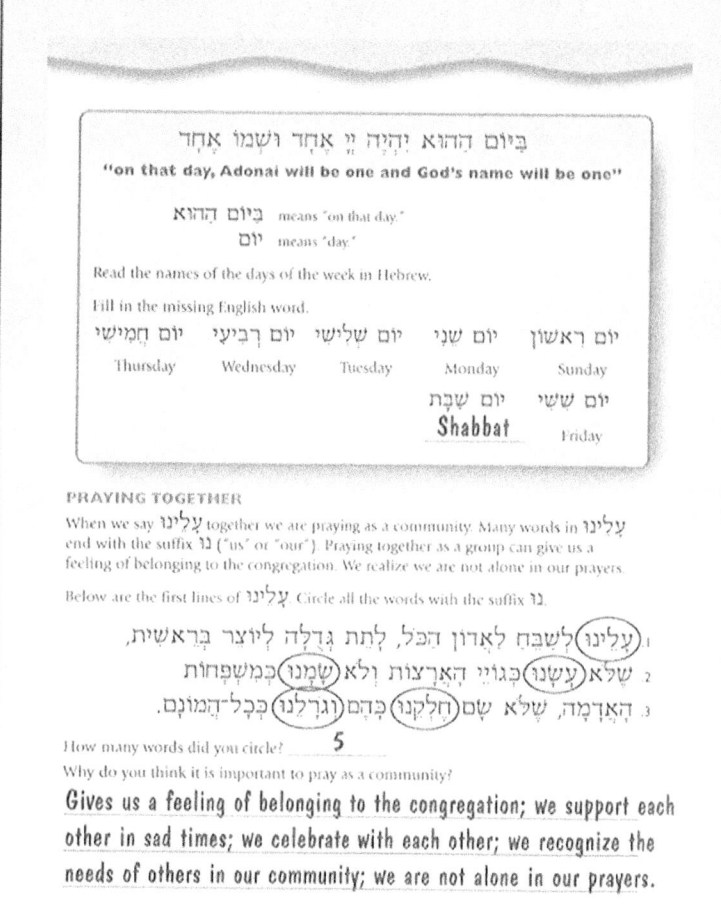

Call on students to read aloud the circled words in lines 1–3 as well as each complete line.

A Musical Note

Teach the students to chant Aleinu.

Have students stand, chant the prayer, bend their knees, and bow at the appropriate place.

AN ETHICAL ECHO

What does "image" mean? (*reflection; how people see us*)

What image do we want to project, beyond our physical features? (*kindness; trustworthiness; honesty; reliability*)

Read the paragraph with the students.

THINK ABOUT THIS!

Read the section and discuss the following questions:

- Why is it sometimes hard for us to treat everyone with the same respect and tolerance? (*we feel superior; we want everyone to be the same; we don't accept differences in people's looks or ideas*)

- What do you think the expression "beauty is only skin deep" means? (*it is not important how a person looks, but rather how he or she acts toward others; a physically beautiful person may not behave beautifully*)

- Can you think of other expressions that have the same message? (*"you can't judge a book by its cover"; "beauty is in the eye of the beholder"; "he/she has inner beauty"*)

Photo Op

Call on a student to read the caption.

Bring a mirror to class. Have students look in the mirror and name one physical and one nonphysical attribute about themselves. Examples: "I have freckles and I like cats" or "I have short, brown hair and I'm scared of heights."

FLUENT READING

Read together the lines the class has already studied (lines 1, 4–5, 11–12).

Call on individual students to read the complete prayer.

A Musical Note

Teach the students to sing the complete prayer.

WORKSHEET

Duplicate and hand out copies of the worksheet for Lesson 6 to review skills and concepts.

FAMILY EDUCATION

Duplicate and send home copies of "As a Family: Showing Respect for God" (at the back of this guide) if you did not already do so.

FLUENT READING

Practice reading the following verses from עָלֵינוּ.

1. עָלֵינוּ לְשַׁבֵּחַ לַאֲדוֹן הַכֹּל, לָתֵת גְּדֻלָּה לְיוֹצֵר בְּרֵאשִׁית,
2. שֶׁלֹּא עָשָׂנוּ כְּגוֹיֵי הָאֲרָצוֹת וְלֹא שָׂמָנוּ כְּמִשְׁפְּחוֹת
3. הָאֲדָמָה, שֶׁלֹּא שָׂם חֶלְקֵנוּ כָּהֶם, וְגוֹרָלֵנוּ כְּכָל-הֲמוֹנָם.
4. וַאֲנַחְנוּ כּוֹרְעִים וּמִשְׁתַּחֲוִים וּמוֹדִים
5. לִפְנֵי מֶלֶךְ מַלְכֵי הַמְּלָכִים, הַקָּדוֹשׁ בָּרוּךְ הוּא,
6. שֶׁהוּא נוֹטֶה שָׁמַיִם וְיוֹסֵד אָרֶץ, וּמוֹשַׁב יְקָרוֹ בַּשָּׁמַיִם
7. מִמַּעַל, וּשְׁכִינַת עֻזּוֹ בְּגָבְהֵי מְרוֹמִים. הוּא אֱלֹהֵינוּ, אֵין
8. עוֹד. אֱמֶת מַלְכֵּנוּ, אֶפֶס זוּלָתוֹ, כַּכָּתוּב בְּתוֹרָתוֹ: וְיָדַעְתָּ
9. הַיּוֹם וַהֲשֵׁבֹתָ אֶל לְבָבֶךָ, כִּי יְיָ הוּא הָאֱלֹהִים בַּשָּׁמַיִם
10. מִמַּעַל וְעַל הָאָרֶץ מִתָּחַת, אֵין עוֹד.
11. וְנֶאֱמַר: וְהָיָה יְיָ לְמֶלֶךְ עַל כָּל-הָאָרֶץ, בַּיּוֹם הַהוּא
12. יִהְיֶה יְיָ אֶחָד וּשְׁמוֹ אֶחָד.

LESSON 6
Worksheet

Name: _____

עָלֵינוּ

1. Write the English meaning on the line next to each Hebrew word or phrase below.

   it is our duty   and we   to praise   God   Ruler of rulers   and thank

   לְשַׁבֵּחַ _____   מֶלֶךְ מַלְכֵי הַמְּלָכִים _____

   וַאֲנַחְנוּ _____   עָלֵינוּ _____

   אָדוֹן _____   וּמוֹדִים _____

2. The English phrases below are in the same order as in עָלֵינוּ. The Hebrew phrases are mixed up. Indicate the correct order of the Hebrew phrases by writing the number of the matching English next to each.

   (1) It is our duty to praise the God of all.
   (2) and we bend the knee, bow, and give thanks
   (3) before the Ruler of rulers
   (4) On that day God will be One and God's name will be One.

   ____ וַאֲנַחְנוּ כּוֹרְעִים וּמִשְׁתַּחֲוִים וּמוֹדִים
   ____ בַּיּוֹם הַהוּא יִהְיֶה יְיָ אֶחָד וּשְׁמוֹ אֶחָד
   ____ עָלֵינוּ לְשַׁבֵּחַ לַאֲדוֹן הַכֹּל
   ____ לִפְנֵי מֶלֶךְ מַלְכֵי הַמְּלָכִים

3. Why do we bend our knees and bow during עָלֵינוּ?

   _____

4. Why is עָלֵינוּ a "pledge of loyalty" to God?

   _____
   _____

HINENI—THE NEW HEBREW THROUGH PRAYER 3 © Behrman House Publishers

LESSON 7 קָדִישׁ

LEARNING OBJECTIVES

Prayer Reading Skills
- The roots ברכ ("bless" or "praise"); מלכ ("rule"); גדל ("great"); קדשׁ ("holy"); שׁלמ ("peace")
- Recognizing similarities between Aramaic and Hebrew
- Recognizing the prayer עֹשֶׂה שָׁלוֹם

Prayer Concepts
There are several versions of the Kaddish. The Kaddish divides sections of the service. The Mourner's Kaddish:

- is written mostly in Aramaic.
- is recited in memory of someone who has died.
- does not mention death.
- is a prayer in praise of God.
- concludes with the prayer for peace, עֹשֶׂה שָׁלוֹם.
- traditionally ends with the mourner stepping back and bowing as if leaving the presence of a ruler.
- is recited in the presence of a *minyan*.

BEYOND THE TEXTBOOK
The term נִחוּם אֲבֵלִים ("comforting mourners")

The rituals of death and mourning

ABOUT THE PRAYER
The Kaddish is a prayer written almost entirely in Aramaic, a language related to Hebrew. It divides sections of the service. There are several versions of the Kaddish. The last sentence of the Reader's Kaddish and the Mourner's Kaddish is the Hebrew prayer עֹשֶׂה שָׁלוֹם. A shorter Kaddish is known as the half Kaddish. The Mourner's Kaddish is recited in memory of those who have died.

INSTRUCTIONAL MATERIALS
Text pages 68–77

Word Cards 70–82

Worksheet 7

Family Education: "As a Family: In Memory" (at the back of this guide)

SET INDUCTION
Initiate a discussion with the students about their Hebrew names. If they were named after someone in their family, have them find out about those family members—their names, occupations, countries of origin.

Class Discussion
Explain that memory—זִכָּרוֹן—is an important part of the Jewish tradition. Through memory we keep the past alive. The Jewish people have collective memories—memories of events that affected all of our people. The Kiddush reminds us that Shabbat is a "memory of the work of creation" (זִכָּרוֹן לְמַעֲשֵׂה בְרֵאשִׁית) and a "memory of the going out from Egypt" (זֵכֶר לִיצִיאַת מִצְרַיִם). The Passover seder is a memory of the Jews' lives as slaves in Egypt and of the Exodus. Israeli Remembrance Day (יוֹם הַזִּכָּרוֹן) pays tribute to the soldiers who died defending their country. Yom Hashoah (יוֹם הַשׁוֹאָה) honors the memory of those who died in the Holocaust.

Tell the students that each of our families has personal memories, too, with rituals and traditions to keep those memories alive.

- Call on students to give their Hebrew names. If they were named after someone, have students give the name and something about the person.
- Ask: When do people call us by our Hebrew names? (*in Hebrew school; at a brit milah, baby naming, and Bar and Bat Mitzvah; in an aliyah to the Torah; on the ketubah and in the marriage ceremony; at the burial ceremony and on the gravestone*)
- Bring a *yahrzeit* candle to class. Explain that we light a memorial candle like it on the anniversary of a loved one's death. Visit the sanctuary to view the memorial wall and the lit lights indicating the *yahrzeit* of those who have died.

As a Family
You might wish to send home copies of the page "As a Family: In Memory" with the students at this time.

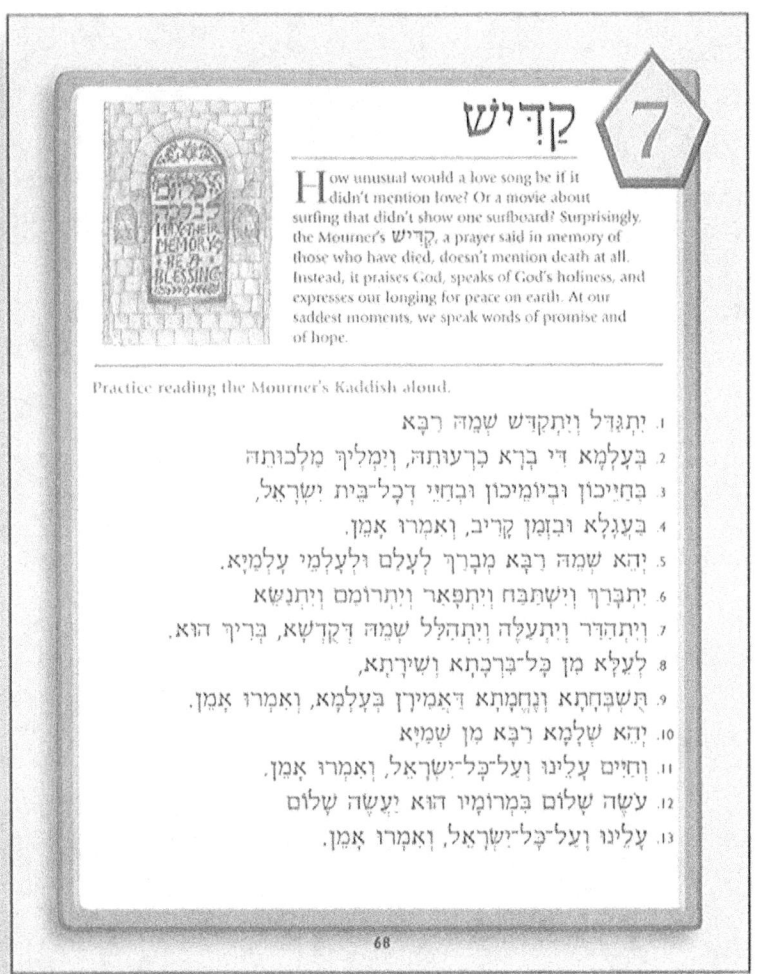

Have half of the class read וְיִתְ aloud and the other half read the remainder of each word.

Switch reading roles. Then select individuals to follow the same procedure.

Call on students to read lines 6–7.

Lines 12–13

Direct the students to read lines 12–13. Ask if they recognize the Hebrew prayer that concludes the Kaddish. (*Oseh Shalom*) Call on students to read the lines.

Practice reading the entire prayer with the students.

INTO THE TEXT

Read the introduction to the lesson aloud with the students.

Ask: How can reciting the Mourner's Kaddish connect you with the person who has died? (*brings back memories; acknowledges that each generation says Kaddish in memory of loved ones*)

Display Word Card 70, קָדִישׁ. Ask:

- What is the root of the word? (קדשׁ)
- What do words built on this root mean? (*holy, sanctify*)

Reading Practice

There are five paragraphs in the Mourner's Kaddish. Have students circle the first word in lines 1, 5, 6, 10, and 12. Each of these lines begins a new paragraph. Then have students number the English lines 1–13 on page 69 and circle the first word in the English lines 1, 5, 6, 10, and 12.

Write the phrase וְאִמְרוּ אָמֵן ("and say, Amen") on the chalkboard. Four of the paragraphs in the Mourner's Kaddish conclude with the phrase וְאִמְרוּ אָמֵן. Direct the students to lightly circle the phrase in both the Hebrew and English versions (lines 4, 9, 11, 13).

Line 5

In some congregations, only mourners stand to recite the Mourner's Kaddish. They recite lines 1–4, the congregation joins in for line 5, and only the mourners continue with lines 6–13.

Have the students read line 5 aloud individually and then in unison.

Lines 6–7

Ask: What word in line 7 is built on the root קדשׁ ("holy")? (דְּקֻדְשָׁא)

Write the word-part וְיִתְ on the chalkboard and draw a box around it. Next to it, write the following list of word-parts in a column.

פָּאַר
רוֹמֵם
נַשֵּׂא
הַדֵּר
עַלֶּה
הַלֵּל

Photo Op

Call on a student to read the caption. Mention that offering comfort to the mourner is a mitzvah. Introduce the phrase נִחוּם אֲבֵלִים, "comforting mourners."

Ask: How can we offer comfort to mourners? (*attend the funeral service; visit during shiva; listen quietly if the mourner wants to talk about the loss; offer to help with daily obligations such as shopping and cooking; send a sympathy card; make a donation in memory of the deceased; plant a tree in Israel in memory of the deceased*)

Why is it also important to *us* to offer comfort to those who have suffered a loss? (*we are fulfilling a mitzvah; it opens our minds and hearts to the suffering of others; it connects us to the community*)

Judaism teaches us the importance of comforting those who have suffered a loss, for them and for us.

May God's name be great and may it be made holy
in the world created according to God's will. May God rule
in our own lives and our own days, and in the life of all the house of Israel,
swiftly and soon, and say, Amen.
May God's great name be blessed forever and ever.
Blessed, praised, glorified, exalted, extolled,
honored, magnified, and adored be the name of the Holy One, blessed is God,
though God is beyond all the blessings, songs,
adorations, and consolations that are spoken in the world, and say, Amen.
May there be great peace from heaven
and life for us and for all Israel, and say, Amen.
May God who makes peace in the heavens, make peace
for us and for all Israel. And say, Amen.

DID YOU KNOW?

Read the explanation with the students.

Aramaic is an ancient Semitic language related to Hebrew. There are other Aramaic prayers, such as Kol Nidre, which we recite on Yom Kippur.

PRAYER DICTIONARY

Display the following Word Cards in random order: 70, 72, 74, 75, 76, 78, 80, 81.

Challenge the students to put them in sets according to their roots.

Students should read the words in each set, and name the root for each set and its meaning.

(70, 72: קדשׁ ["holy"]; 74, 78: עלם ["world" or " forever"]; 75, 76: מלב ["rule"]; 80, 81: ברכ ["bless" or " praise"])

Word Find

Display Word Cards 71–82 in random order.

Ask twelve students to each select one Word Card. Direct them to find their word in the prayer on page 68, and to read the Word Card and then the complete line aloud.

THE HEBREW-ARAMAIC CONNECTION

Call on students to read aloud the words in each column before beginning the exercise.

Have the class complete the exercise individually, then call on students to read each matching word set aloud (for example, גָּדְלָה, יִתְגַּדַּל).

ROOT SEARCH

Call on students to read the Aramaic words aloud. Have the class work in pairs to complete the exercise. Review the answers together.

Ask: Which words in the list share the same root? (קַדִּישׁ, וְיִתְקַדַּשׁ; מַלְכוּתֵהּ, וְיַמְלִיךְ; בְּרִיךְ, בִּרְכָתָא)

Ask what the general meaning is for each set of words.

The Fruit of the Tree

Create two fruit trees with the roots שלמ ("peace") and גדל ("great").

Add fruit to the trees using words from the Hebrew-Aramaic Connection on page 70 and the Root Search on page 71.

Fruit Salad

Review all the roots the students have learned.

Remove the fruit from all the trees you have made. Mix up the fruit in a bowl to create a "fruit salad." Challenge the students to sort out the fruit according to their roots and place them back on the correct tree. Have students read the word on each fruit as they replace it on the tree.

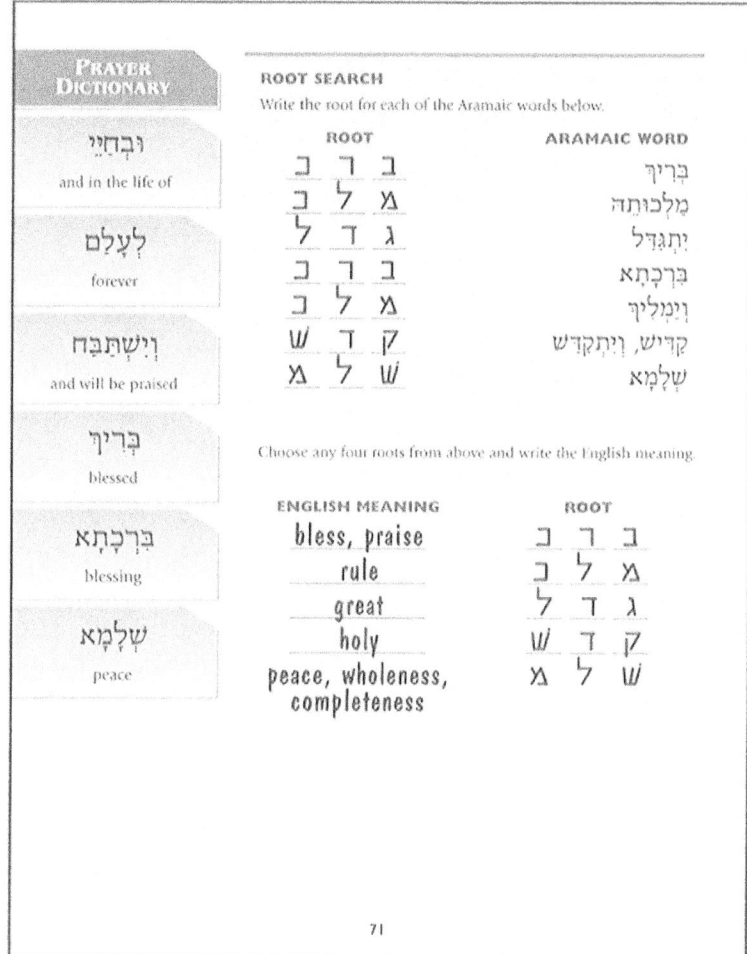

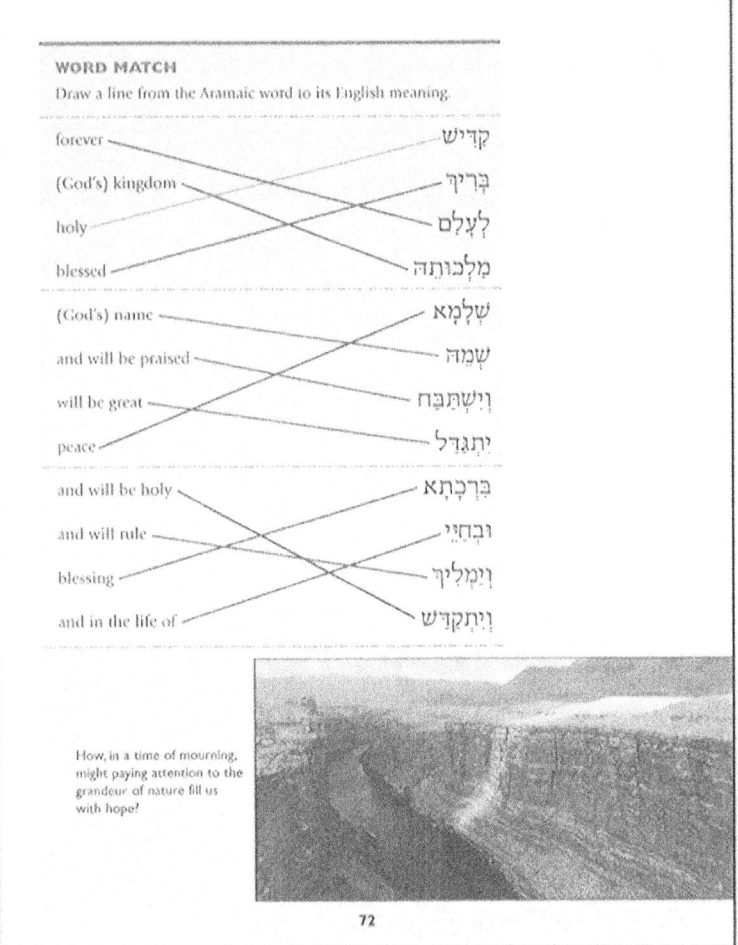

WORD MATCH

Have students complete the activity individually and check one another's answers. Walk around the class to oversee their cooperative work.

Photo Op

Call on a student to read the caption. Pose the following questions:

- What does the term "grandeur" mean? (*splendor; magnificence; vastness*)
- What places or settings might fit that description? (*Grand Canyon; Niagara Falls; sunset; the ocean; mountain peaks; great valleys*)
- How might the grandeur of nature fill the mourner with hope? (*it is a reminder that there is still beauty in the world; the grandeur of a scene can lift the spirit and offer hope and optimism*)

THE THEME OF THE PRAYER

Read the introduction together. Allow the students at least 10 minutes to read the English translation and complete the exercise independently. Review the answers together.

THE THEME OF THE PRAYER

We have learned that the Mourner's Kaddish is said in memory of someone who has died, yet it contains no mention of death.

Reread the English translation of the Kaddish on page 69. Pay attention to the tone and mood of the prayer. Then do the following exercise.

1. Fill in the blank by choosing the correct word.
   The Kaddish is a prayer of __praise__ to God. (thanks/praise/request)

2. Choose four words from the English translation of the prayer that illustrate your answer to number 1.
   __glorified   exalted   extolled   honored (etc.)__

3. The Kaddish ends on a hopeful, optimistic note.
   It ends with a wish for __peace__.
   Why do you think the Kaddish ends with this wish?
   __We wish for peace for ourselves, for our community, and for all the world.__

4. Why do you think the Kaddish is recited by mourners even though it does not mention death?
   __We praise God even when we are sad; we find comfort in God; at our saddest moments we speak words of promise and hope.__

KADDISH QUIZ

Practice reading the Kaddish as a class. Have the students complete the quiz on the next page.

KADDISH QUIZ

Read the קַדִּישׁ and find the answers to the questions that appear on the opposite page.

1. יִתְגַּדַּל וְיִתְקַדַּשׁ שְׁמֵהּ רַבָּא
2. בְּעָלְמָא דִּי בְרָא כִרְעוּתֵהּ, וְיַמְלִיךְ מַלְכוּתֵהּ
3. בְּחַיֵּיכוֹן וּבְיוֹמֵיכוֹן וּבְחַיֵּי דְכָל־בֵּית יִשְׂרָאֵל,
4. בַּעֲגָלָא וּבִזְמַן קָרִיב, וְאִמְרוּ אָמֵן.
5. יְהֵא שְׁמֵהּ רַבָּא מְבָרַךְ לְעָלַם וּלְעָלְמֵי עָלְמַיָּא.
6. יִתְבָּרַךְ וְיִשְׁתַּבַּח וְיִתְפָּאַר וְיִתְרוֹמַם וְיִתְנַשֵּׂא
7. וְיִתְהַדָּר וְיִתְעַלֶּה וְיִתְהַלָּל שְׁמֵהּ דְּקֻדְשָׁא בְּרִיךְ הוּא.
8. לְעֵלָּא מִן כָּל־בִּרְכָתָא וְשִׁירָתָא,
9. תֻּשְׁבְּחָתָא וְנֶחֱמָתָא דַּאֲמִירָן בְּעָלְמָא, וְאִמְרוּ אָמֵן.
10. יְהֵא שְׁלָמָא רַבָּא מִן שְׁמַיָּא
11. וְחַיִּים עָלֵינוּ וְעַל־כָּל־יִשְׂרָאֵל, וְאִמְרוּ אָמֵן.
12. עֹשֶׂה שָׁלוֹם בִּמְרוֹמָיו הוּא יַעֲשֶׂה שָׁלוֹם
13. עָלֵינוּ וְעַל־כָּל־יִשְׂרָאֵל, וְאִמְרוּ אָמֵן.

Consider using the Kaddish Quiz for review or assessment to check student progress. You may wish to check their answers privately, then review as a class. Or pair up students and allow them to work together to complete the quiz.

1. Circle all the words in the קָדִישׁ that have the root קדשׁ.
   How many words did you circle? __2__
   What does the root קדשׁ mean? __holy__

2. Put a star above all the words with the root ברכ.
   How many words did you star? __4__
   What does the root ברכ mean? __praise, bless__

3. Three words in the קָדִישׁ mean "life." Write them here.
   בְּחַיֵּיכוֹן   וּבְחַיֵּי   וְחַיִּים

4. Peace is an important concept in the קָדִישׁ. Write the Hebrew word for "peace." __שָׁלוֹם__
   This word—or a variation—appears three times near the end of the קָדִישׁ. Put a box around each one.

5. We know that כָּל means __all__
   Now underline כָּל or כֹּל wherever it appears.
   How many underlined words do you have? __4__

6. עוֹלָם means "forever" or "world." This word appears five times, in a variety of forms, in the קָדִישׁ.
   Write the five words here.
   בְּעָלְמָא   לְעָלַם   וּלְעָלְמֵי
   עָלְמַיָּא   בְּעָלְמָא

> **ABOUT THE KADDISH**
>
> In this chapter we have learned about the Mourner's קָדִישׁ. But there are other versions of the קָדִישׁ, for example the חֲצִי קָדִישׁ ("half Kaddish"), which is only slightly shorter. The קָדִישׁ divides up the service, almost the way a file divider separates the subjects in your school binder. It indicates the end of one section of the service and the beginning of the next.
>
> We are not sure who wrote the קָדִישׁ or when. It probably developed over hundreds of years. We do know that almost 800 years ago the קָדִישׁ came to be the prayer said by mourners.
>
> In some congregations, only the mourners and those observing yahrzeit—the anniversary of a loved one's death—stand as they recite the קָדִישׁ. In other congregations, everyone stands as a sign of support for the mourners and to remember those who died in the Holocaust.
>
> We say the קָדִישׁ only in the presence of a מִנְיָן. As the mourners rhythmically chant the prayer, the congregation publicly acknowledges God's greatness. Although the Mourner's קָדִישׁ is recited in memory of the dead, its words also give strength to the living.
>
> Below are the last two lines of the קָדִישׁ.
>
> עֹשֶׂה שָׁלוֹם בִּמְרוֹמָיו הוּא יַעֲשֶׂה שָׁלוֹם
> עָלֵינוּ וְעַל־כָּל־יִשְׂרָאֵל, וְאִמְרוּ אָמֵן.
>
> *May God who makes peace in the heavens, make peace for us and for all Israel. And say, Amen.*
>
> עֹשֶׂה שָׁלוֹם is the same sentence that concludes both the עֲמִידָה and בִּרְכַּת הַמָּזוֹן (Grace After Meals). When we say עֹשֶׂה שָׁלוֹם at the end of the קָדִישׁ and the עֲמִידָה, it is traditional to take three steps backward, then to bow to the left, to the right, and then forward. It is as if the person praying is leaving the presence of a king or a queen. Who is the Ruler whose presence we are leaving? __God__.
>
> Answer the following questions in Hebrew.
>
> 1. In עֹשֶׂה שָׁלוֹם, what do we ask God for? __שָׁלוֹם__
> 2. For whom do we want peace? __עָלֵינוּ וְעַל כָּל יִשְׂרָאֵל__
>
> 76

Extending the Lesson

Discuss Jewish rituals regarding death and mourning. Many of our rituals reflect the traditions of our ancestors as described in the Torah.

- Burial (Sarah in the Cave of Machpelah, Genesis 23:1–2, 7–20); Jacob among his own people, Genesis 47:29–31)
- *K'riah*: tearing of cloth (Jacob mourning his son Joseph, whom he thought had been killed, Genesis 37:34–35)
- *Shiva*: mourning for seven days (Joseph mourning Jacob, Genesis 50:10)
- *Sh'loshim*: mourning for thirty days (the Israelites mourning Moses, Deuteronomy 34:8)

ABOUT THE KADDISH

Read the first paragraph with the students. Direct them to the prayer on page 68 or 74 (their choice). Explain that the half Kaddish is comprised of lines 1–9. The half Kaddish is a *doxology*—an expression of praise to God which separates parts of a prayer service.

Read the second and third paragraphs on page 76. Discuss the custom in your synagogue when reciting the Mourner's Kaddish.

Read the fourth paragraph. Remind the students that a *minyan* is a community of ten or more Jewish adults.

Ask: In what ways do the words of the Kaddish give strength to the living? (*gives emotional support because the Kaddish is recited in the presence of the community; reminds the mourner that others have suffered loss, too; reminds us that all life is ephemeral and impermanent*)

עֹשֶׂה שָׁלוֹם

Read the explanation and have the students complete the questions at the bottom of the page.

Recite עֹשֶׂה שָׁלוֹם with the students.

Explain that we do not *sing* עֹשֶׂה שָׁלוֹם at the conclusion of the Mourner's Kaddish, we simply recite it.

Prayer Reading

Ask the class to stand and recite the Mourner's Kaddish together.

FLUENT READING

Divide the class into two teams. Assign one team the odd-numbered lines and the other team the even-numbered lines. Working together, team members should find two words or roots they recognize in each line.

Team members should underline the words, determine their approximate English meaning, and practice reading each complete line.

Score: Award two points for reading the underlined words correctly, two points for the two correct English meanings, and three points for reading the entire line without a mistake.

Top score: Seven points per line (see below).

Number Seven

Talk about the number 7 in Jewish life—the seventh day, Shabbat; seven patriarchs and matriarchs (Abraham, Isaac, Jacob, Sarah, Rebecca, Leah, and Rachel); seven weeks from the Exodus (Passover) to receiving the Torah on Mount Sinai (Shavuot); seven wedding blessings; seven blessings in the Shabbat Amidah; seven days of *shiva*.

WORKSHEET

Duplicate and hand out copies of the worksheet for Lesson 7 to review skills and concepts.

FAMILY EDUCATION

Duplicate and send home copies of "As a Family: In Memory" (at the back of this guide) if you did not already do so.

FLUENT READING

Each line below contains a word or phrase you know. Practice reading the lines.

1. תִּתְגַּדֵּל וְתִתְקַדֵּשׁ בְּתוֹךְ יְרוּשָׁלַיִם עִירְךָ.
2. לְדוֹר וָדוֹר נַגִּיד גָּדְלֶךָ, וּלְנֵצַח נְצָחִים קְדֻשָּׁתְךָ נַקְדִּישׁ.
3. גָּדוֹל יְיָ וּמְהֻלָּל מְאֹד וְלִגְדֻלָּתוֹ אֵין חֵקֶר.
4. וְשִׁבְחֲךָ אֱלֹהֵינוּ מִפִּינוּ לֹא יָמוּשׁ לְעוֹלָם וָעֶד.
5. עָלֵינוּ לְשַׁבֵּחַ לַאֲדוֹן הַכֹּל לָתֵת גְּדֻלָּה לְיוֹצֵר בְּרֵאשִׁית.
6. יְגַדֵּל אֱלֹהִים חַי וְיִשְׁתַּבַּח.
7. מַלְכוּתְךָ מַלְכוּת כָּל עֹלָמִים, וּמֶמְשַׁלְתְּךָ בְּכָל דּוֹר וָדֹר.
8. הַבָּא עָלֵינוּ וְעַל כָּל יִשְׂרָאֵל לְטוֹבָה.
9. כִּי הַמַּלְכוּת שֶׁלְךָ הִיא וּלְעוֹלְמֵי עַד תִּמְלוֹךְ בְּכָבוֹד.
10. בָּרְכוּנִי לְשָׁלוֹם מַלְאֲכֵי הַשָּׁלוֹם מַלְאֲכֵי עֶלְיוֹן.

LESSON 7
Worksheet

Name: _____

קַדִּישׁ

1. What is the root of the word קַדִּישׁ? ___ ___ ___
   Write the English equivalent of the root. _____

2. In what language is most of the קַדִּישׁ written? _____

3. The קַדִּישׁ ends with a short Hebrew prayer. Circle the name of the prayer from the choices below.

   מִי כָמֹכָה   שְׁמַע   עֹשֶׂה שָׁלוֹם   בָּרְכוּ

4. Below are words from the קַדִּישׁ. In the right column, write each word next to its root. In the left column, write the English equivalent of the root.

   דְקֻדְשָׁא   מַלְכוּתֵהּ   יִתְגַּדַּל   שְׁלָמָא   מְבָרַךְ

English	Root	Word
_____	מלכ	_____
_____	שׁלמ	_____
_____	קדשׁ	_____
_____	ברכ	_____
_____	גדל	_____

5. Fill in the missing word in each sentence below.

   • The קַדִּישׁ is recited only in the presence of ten Jewish adults, called a _____.

   • We say the קַדִּישׁ in memory of _____.

   • The קַדִּישׁ is a prayer of _____ to God.

   • The קַדִּישׁ ends on an optimistic note. It ends with a wish for _____.

6. Why do you think the Kaddish is recited by mourners even though it does not mention death?

   _____

   _____

HINENI—THE NEW HEBREW THROUGH PRAYER 3 © Behrman House Publishers

LESSON 8

אֵין כֵּאלֹהֵינוּ

LEARNING OBJECTIVES
Prayer Reading Skills
- The prefixes כ, כְּ ("like"); לְ ("to")
- The suffix נוּ ("our")
- Recognizing related words (e.g., אָדוֹן, אֲדוֹנֵינוּ)
- Recognizing the acrostic אָמֵן

Prayer Concepts
- Ein Keloheinu is a hymn, a song of praise of God.
- Ein Keloheinu is a statement of our belief in God. In it we declare that God is beyond comparison.
- We sing the hymn at the conclusion of the service.

BEYOND THE TEXTBOOK
The term אָמֵן

The family letters כ, כְּ

The term z'mirot

ABOUT THE PRAYER
Ein Keloheinu is a statement of belief in God. In it we refer to different views we have of God—our God, our Sovereign, our Ruler, our Savior. There is a series of themes in the hymn: there is none compared to our God (lines 1–4); we offer thanks to God (lines 5–6); we praise God (lines 7–8); we reaffirm our belief in God (lines 9–10). The words and melody are repeated and are easy to learn.

INSTRUCTIONAL MATERIALS
Text pages 78–85

Word Cards 83–90

Worksheet 8

Family Education: "As a Family: The Roles We Play" (at the back of this guide)

SET INDUCTION
Comparisons
Students often use the phrase "the best." Let's have them think about what that means. Engage the students in the following activity.

Give each student a piece of paper. At the top of the page, have them label three columns Good, Better, and Best.

Students should write the names of five areas of special interest to them in a column down the left side of the page. Examples: sports, movies, ice-cream flavors, books, school subjects, TV shows.

Each student should then fill in three responses for each category—three movies, three books, and so on—writing one response under "Good," another under "Better," and the third under "Best."

Call on the students to share their rating choices.

Discussion
Sometimes we say: "There are no words to describe it. I can't compare it to anything else!" about an experience or event.

Ask: Did you ever have such an experience?

Call on students to describe their experiences.

The Prayer Experience
Many of our prayers use descriptive words for God; for example, when we carry the Torah around the sanctuary (page 22, lines 1–2) and when we recite the Kaddish (page 68, line 6–7). We search for words and then for more words because there really are no words to describe God. God is beyond anything or anyone we can imagine.

Ein Keloheinu—There is None Like Our God—is a hymn, a song in praise of God. This hymn refers to the different ways we honor God. It illustrates our belief that God is beyond comparison.

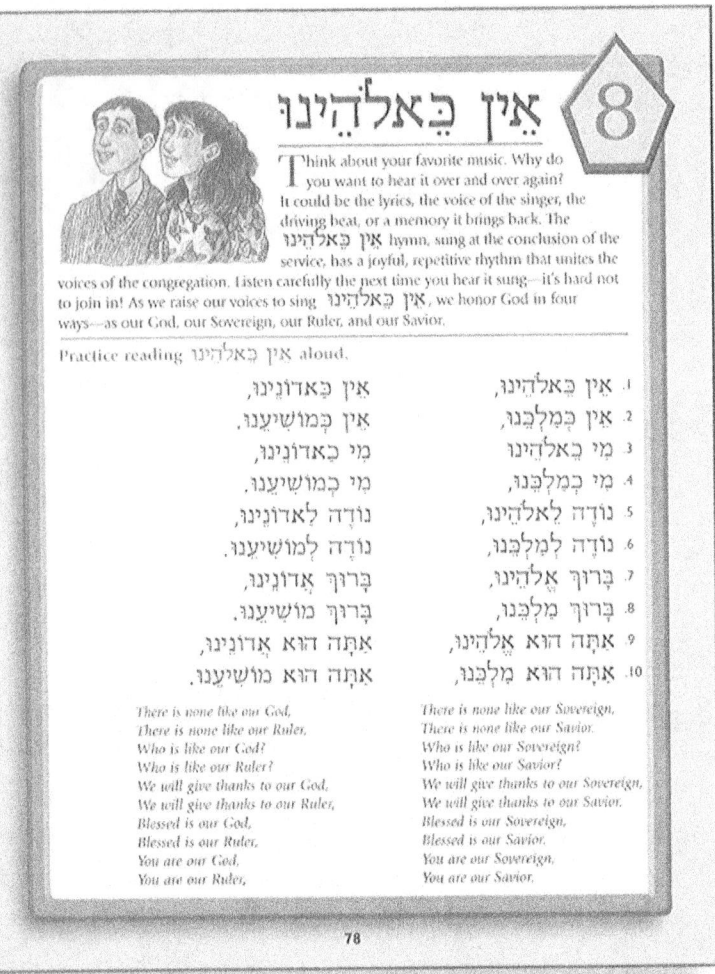

INTO THE TEXT

Read the paragraph aloud with the students.

Direct students to the English translation of the prayer and have them number the lines 1–10.

Call on individuals to read lines 1–2 of the English.

Ask: What four phrases honor God in these lines? (*our God, our Sovereign, our Ruler, our Savior*)

Which phrase indicates that God is beyond all comparison? (*there is none like*)

Reading Practice

Demonstrate the rhythm of the hymn in the following way:

Have students circle the English and Hebrew line numbers 1, 3, 5, 7, 9.

Tell them that each circled line number introduces a new stanza (1–2, 3–4, 5–6, 7–8, 9–10).

Ask the students to count off 1–2–3–4–5, 1–2–3–4–5 around the room.

Each group of five students is responsible for reading one stanza, that is, four phrases, in Hebrew. Each group should then read aloud an English phrase and the corresponding Hebrew phrase in their set of lines.

Rotate each group's assigned lines. Repeat five times until every group has read every stanza.

Think About It

Call on students to read both the English and Hebrew lines 3–4.

Ask: What is the answer to each question in lines 3–4? (*There is none like our God. There is none like our Sovereign. There is none like our Ruler. There is none like our Savior.*)

As a Family

You might wish to send home copies of the "As a Family: The Roles We Play" page at this time.

PRAYER DICTIONARY

Display Word Cards 87–90 in order.

Explain that these are the key words in the prayer. They describe aspects of our relationship with God.

- Have the class read each word in unison, then turn the Word Card over to show the English meaning.
- Ask: What is the common suffix in each word? (נוּ) What is the English meaning of this suffix? (*our*)
- Call on a student to read each word, stopping before the suffix (example: אֱלֹהֵי). The class should read the suffix in unison (נוּ).
- Call on individual students to read each word and say its English meaning.
- Display the Hebrew side of the Word Cards in random order. Call on students to place them in the right-to-left order of the prayer.
- Display the English side of the Word Cards in random order and repeat the activity.

SEARCH AND CIRCLE

Call on students to read each set of words aloud for further reading practice.

Have the class cover the Prayer Dictionary and complete the exercise individually, then uncover it to check their answers.

Photo Op

Call on a student to read the caption.

Ask: What Jewish occasion is depicted in the photo? (*erev Shabbat: candles, ḥallah, wine*)

Introduce the term *z'mirot* (songs we sing after the Shabbat meal). Ask students if they have ever sung *z'mirot* following a Shabbat meal. Talk about the spirit generated when everyone sings lively tunes together.

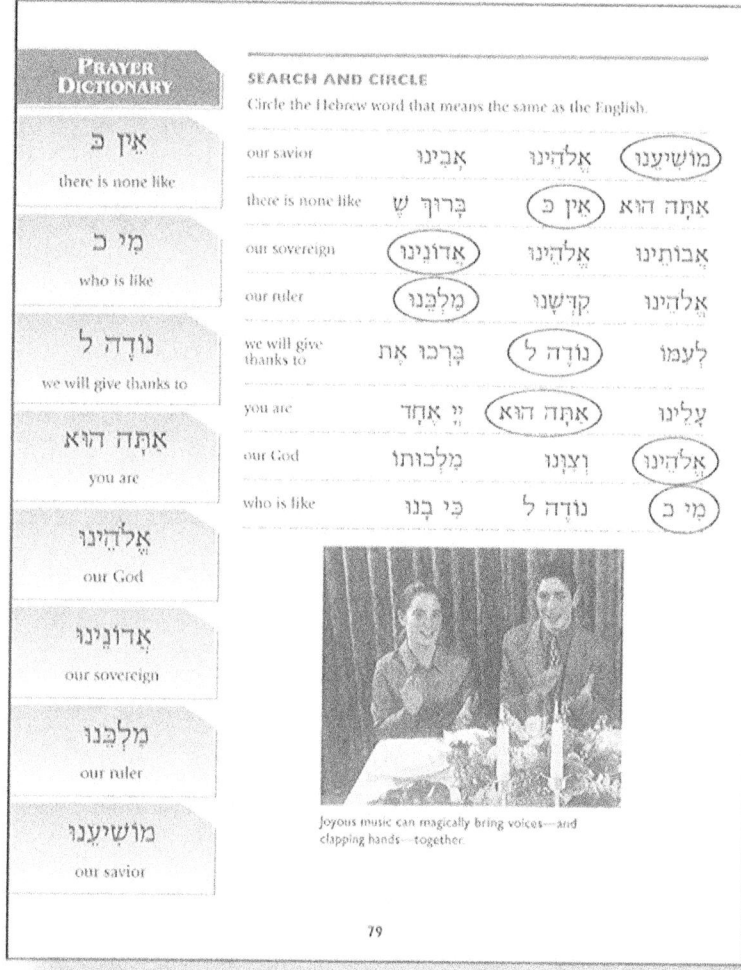

Extending the Opportunity

Invite the rabbi, cantor, or music specialist to class to teach a selection of traditional *z'mirot* to the students.

ARCHITECTURE OF THE PRAYER

Call on a student to read the introductory statement aloud.

Read the prayer aloud in unison with the students rotating lines 1–10 among rows or groups of students.

Have the students complete items 1, 2, and 3 in the exercise.

The Secret Word

Read and complete the exercise at the bottom of the page with the students.

Ask: Why do you think it is appropriate to spell out the word אָמֵן when we sing Ein Keloheinu? (אָמֵן is built on the root meaning "faithful." We are indicating our faith, or belief, in the words just recited. We say אָמֵן at the end of a prayer or blessing and we sing Ein Keloheinu at the end of the service.)

PRAYER BUILDING BLOCKS

אֵין כְּ "there is none like"
מִי כְ "who is like"
נוֹדֶה לְ "we will give thanks to"
אַתָּה הוּא "you are"

Have students complete the three Building Blocks on page 81 and the one on page 82 individually. Walk around the class, checking each student's work.

Practice reading the four phrases in the following ways:

- Say the English meaning of the four phrases in random order.
- Call on students to read the matching Hebrew phrase.
- Repeat, using the Hebrew phrase first, followed by the English.

Partnerships

Direct the students to pair off. One partner is the "teacher" and the other is the "pupil." The "teacher" says the English meaning of each phrase in random order. The "pupil" responds with the correct Hebrew phrase. Repeat, using the Hebrew phrase first, followed by the English. Then have the partners switch roles.

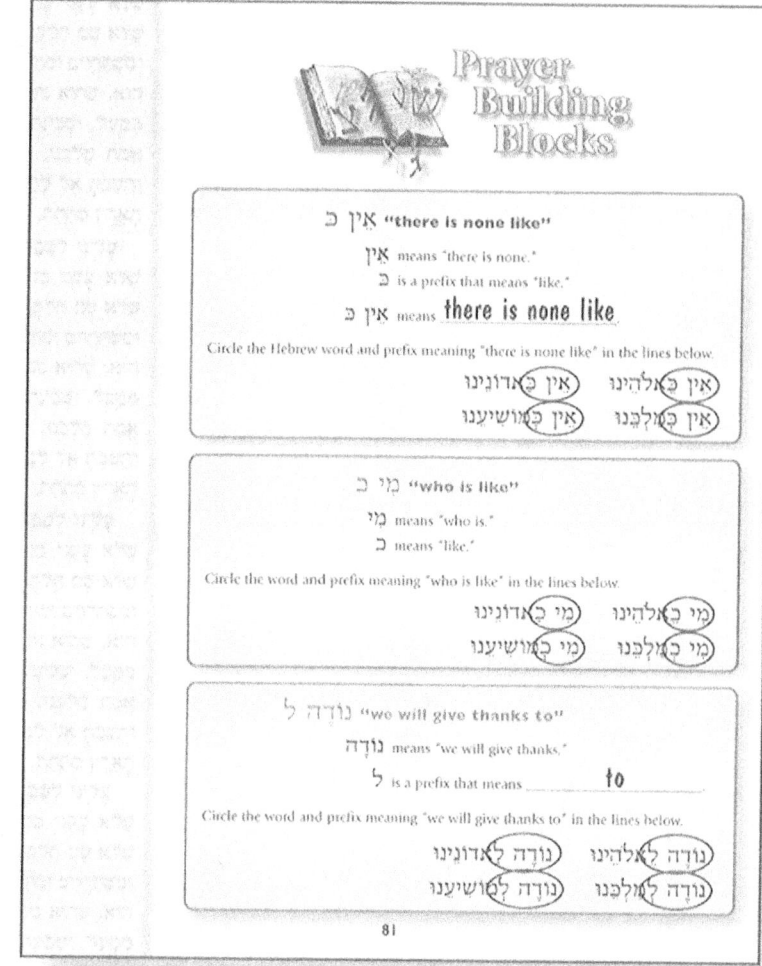

105   LESSON 8

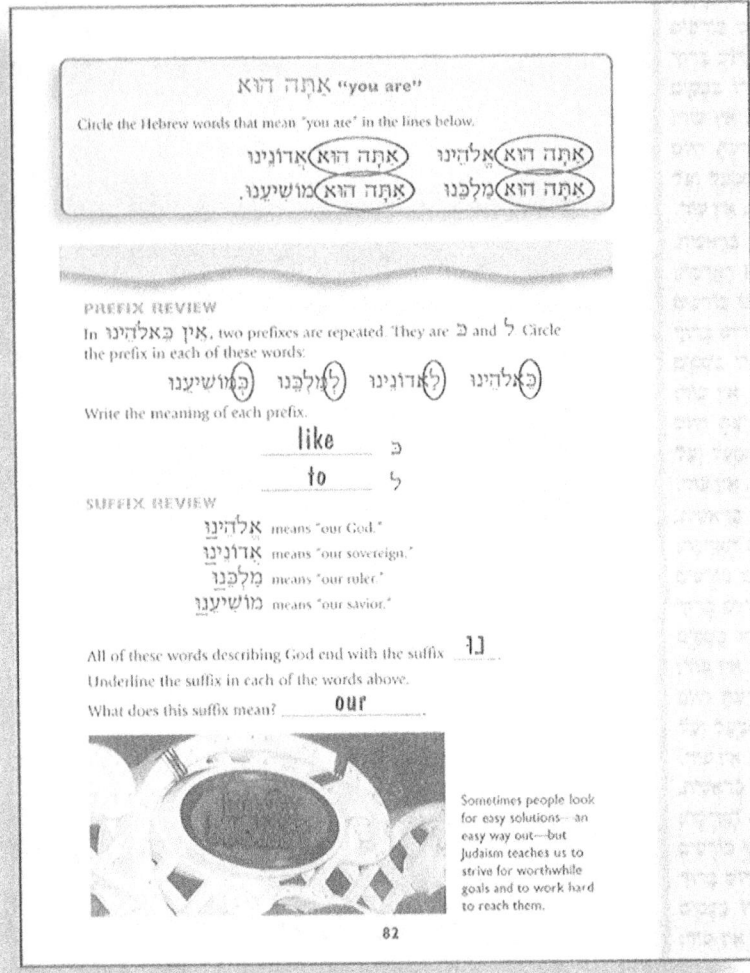

Photo Op

Call on a student to read aloud the caption and the sign in the photo.

Ask: Where do you think the photo was taken? (*Las Vegas; lottery machine; slot machine*)

What does the phrase "easy money" mean? (*not having to work very hard, or at all, to earn money*)

What satisfaction do you get from achieving a goal after working hard? (*you deserve it; you earned it; you did it yourself; you get personal satisfaction*)

Ask the students to share instances in their own lives when they worked to achieve a goal and succeeded.

PREFIX REVIEW

Read the explanation aloud. Explain that the prefixes בּ and כ are the same.

Have students turn to the prayer on page 78. Call on individuals to read each word that begins with the prefix בּ (*lines 1–2*), כ (*lines 3–4*), and ל (*lines 5–6*).

Review the meaning of the prefixes. ("*like,*" "*like,*" or "*to*")

SUFFIX REVIEW

Ask: What is the common suffix in the Hebrew words? (נוּ)

Have students cover the suffix in each word and read aloud the remaining word-part.

Then have them uncover the suffix and read each complete word along with its English meaning.

Display Word Cards 87–90 in random order. Ask for the English meaning of each word.

Have the students complete the exercise individually.

Voice & Echo

Assign half the class to be the Voice and the other half to be the Echo.

Have the students turn to page 78, lines 7–10.

Voices should read the first phrase. Echoes should respond with the next phrase (Voice: בָּרוּךְ אֲדוֹנֵינוּ, Echo: בָּרוּךְ אֱלֹהֵינוּ). Continue this pattern through line 10.

Then read lines 7–10 in unison with the class. Call on individual students to read.

PUTTING IT TOGETHER

Call on students to read the four Hebrew words at the top of the page.

Have the students follow the directions.

Read the explanation to the second part of the page with the students.

Allow a few minutes for them to complete the activity.

Call on individual students to read each set of words aloud and to give the English meaning for the word in column 1.

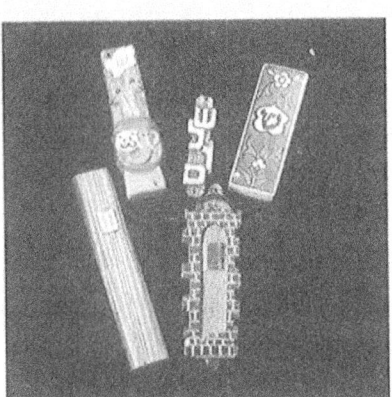

A HYMN OF PRAISE

Read the explanation aloud.

Remind students that a hymn is a song praising God.

Allow the students several minutes to consider the question and write their answers on the blank lines.

Call on individuals to share their insights with the class.

A Musical Note

Teach the students to sing אֵין כֵּאלֹהֵינוּ.

Photo Op

Call on a student to read the caption. Ask the following questions:

- What does a mezuzah represent? (*a Jewish home; pride in one's Jewish identity*)
- Which letter appears on the mezuzah? (שׁ)
- The letter שׁ represents God's name, שַׁדַּי, Almighty. The three Hebrew letters that make up שַׁדַּי are also the initial letters of the Hebrew words שׁוֹמֵר דַּלְתוֹת יִשְׂרָאֵל ("Guardian of the doors of Israel"). Why is that an appropriate name to put on the mezuzah? (*the mezuzah is affixed to the doorpost, gateway to the house; people believe that God will protect homes that have a mezuzah*)
- When God's name שַׁדַּי first appears in the Torah, God is making a covenant—*brit*—with Abraham (Genesis 17:1–10). Based on that, why do you think שַׁדַּי is appropriate for the mezuzah? (*the Jewish people living in the home are part of the covenant*)
- What statement of belief is found inside the mezuzah? (*the Sh'ma*)

FLUENT READING

Instruct each student to trace the outline of his or her hand on a sheet of paper, and number the fingers 1–5.

Have students choose five lines on page 85 and write one number in each finger. As they read each line correctly, they should draw a *Magen David*—a Jewish Star—on the finger with that number in their drawing.

Alternative: Students might enjoy playing the game with a partner. In that case, have them each draw both hands and number the fingers 1–10. As they read a line correctly to each other, they draw a *Magen David* on the finger with that number. Their partner corrects any reading errors. Partners can take turns reading the ten lines in the order they choose.

WORKSHEET

Duplicate and hand out copies of the worksheet for Lesson 8 to review skills and concepts.

FAMILY EDUCATION

Duplicate and send home copies of "As a Family: The Roles We Play" (at the back of this guide) if you did not do so earlier.

FLUENT READING

Each line below contains a word you know. Practice reading the lines.

1. מִי כַיְיָ אֱלֹהֵינוּ, הַמַּגְבִּיהִי לָשָׁבֶת.
2. אָבִינוּ מַלְכֵּנוּ, שְׁמַע קוֹלֵנוּ.
3. אֵין גְּדֻלָּה כַּתּוֹרָה וְאֵין דּוֹרְשֶׁיהָ כְּיִשְׂרָאֵל.
4. הוּא מַלְכֵּנוּ. הוּא מוֹשִׁיעֵנוּ.
5. בָּרְכֵנוּ אָבִינוּ כֻּלָּנוּ כְּאֶחָד בְּאוֹר פָּנֶיךָ.
6. אֵין אַדִּיר כַּיְיָ, וְאֵין בָּרוּךְ כְּבֶן עַמְרָם.
7. אֶחָד הוּא אֱלֹהֵינוּ. הוּא אָבִינוּ.
8. בָּרוּךְ אַתָּה, יְיָ אֱלֹהֵינוּ, מֶלֶךְ הָעוֹלָם. הָאֵל, אָבִינוּ, מַלְכֵּנוּ.
9. אָבִינוּ מַלְכֵּנוּ, חַדֵּשׁ עָלֵינוּ שָׁנָה טוֹבָה.
10. שְׁמַע יִשְׂרָאֵל: יְיָ אֱלֹהֵינוּ, יְיָ אֶחָד.

LESSON 8
Worksheet

Name: _____

אֵין כֵּאלֹהֵינוּ

1. What is the meaning of the suffix נוּ in the following words? _____

   מַלְכֵּנוּ   מוֹשִׁיעֵנוּ   אֱלֹהֵינוּ   אֲדוֹנֵינוּ

   Which of these words has the root "rule"? Write it here. _____

2. Write the number of the English phrase next to the matching Hebrew.

   (1) there is none   מִי _____
   (2) who is   אַתָּה הוּא _____
   (3) we will give thanks   אֵין _____
   (4) blessed is   בָּרוּךְ _____
   (5) you are   נוֹדֶה _____

3. Circle the prefix in each Hebrew word below. Then draw a line to connect the prefix to its English meaning in the phrase below it.

   כֵּאלֹהֵינוּ   כַּאדוֹנֵינוּ   לְמַלְכֵּנוּ
   like our God   like our Sovereign   to our Ruler

4. The English phrases below are in the same order as in אֵין כֵּאלֹהֵינוּ. The Hebrew phrases are mixed up. Indicate the correct order of the Hebrew phrases by writing the number of the matching English next to each.

   1. There is none like our God,   2. There is none like our Sovereign,
   3. There is none like our Ruler,   4. There is none like our Savior.

   _____ אֵין כְּמוֹשִׁיעֵנוּ   _____ אֵין כַּאדוֹנֵינוּ
   _____ אֵין כֵּאלֹהֵינוּ   _____ אֵין כְּמַלְכֵּנוּ

5. Explain the theme of אֵין כֵּאלֹהֵינוּ in your own words. _____

LESSON 9
הַשְׁכִּיבֵנוּ \ שְׁמַע \ מוֹדָה אֲנִי

LEARNING OBJECTIVES

Prayer Reading Skills
- The root עמד ("stand")
- Recognizing related words (e.g., שָׁלוֹם, שְׁלוֹמֶךָ)

Prayer Concepts

Hashkiveinu:
- is the second blessing after the Sh'ma in the evening service.
- asks that God shelter us with peace and protect us during the night.

Sh'ma:
- affirms our belief in one God.
- is our pledge of allegiance to God.
- is often recited with our eyes closed to avoid distractions.
- is recited during the prayer service, and in our homes at night and in the morning.

Modeh Ani:
- is recited in the morning when we wake up.
- thanks God for returning our souls to us and giving us a new day.
- expresses the belief that God is faithful and compassionate toward us.

BEYOND THE TEXTBOOK

The root שלם ("peace," "wholeness," or "completeness")

Holiday connection: Sukkot

The vowels יִ , ֵ , ֶ

ABOUT THE PRAYER

Hashkiveinu, Sh'ma, and Modeh Ani form a cycle of prayers for sleeping and waking. Hashkiveinu, recited in the evening service, asks for God's protection from harm during the night. The Sh'ma, recited in the synagogue and at home both in the evening and in the morning, affirms our belief in one God. Modeh Ani, a prayer we say at home upon awakening in the morning, thanks God for returning our souls to us and giving us the gift of a new day.

INSTRUCTIONAL MATERIALS

Text pages 86–93

Word Cards 6, 91–99

Worksheet 9

Family Education: "As a Family: Shelter of Peace" (at the back of this guide)

SET INDUCTION

Ask students to recount instances when they felt more apprehensive in the night about an upcoming event. Did they have a different attitude in the morning? You may wish to get the discussion underway by giving an example of your own.

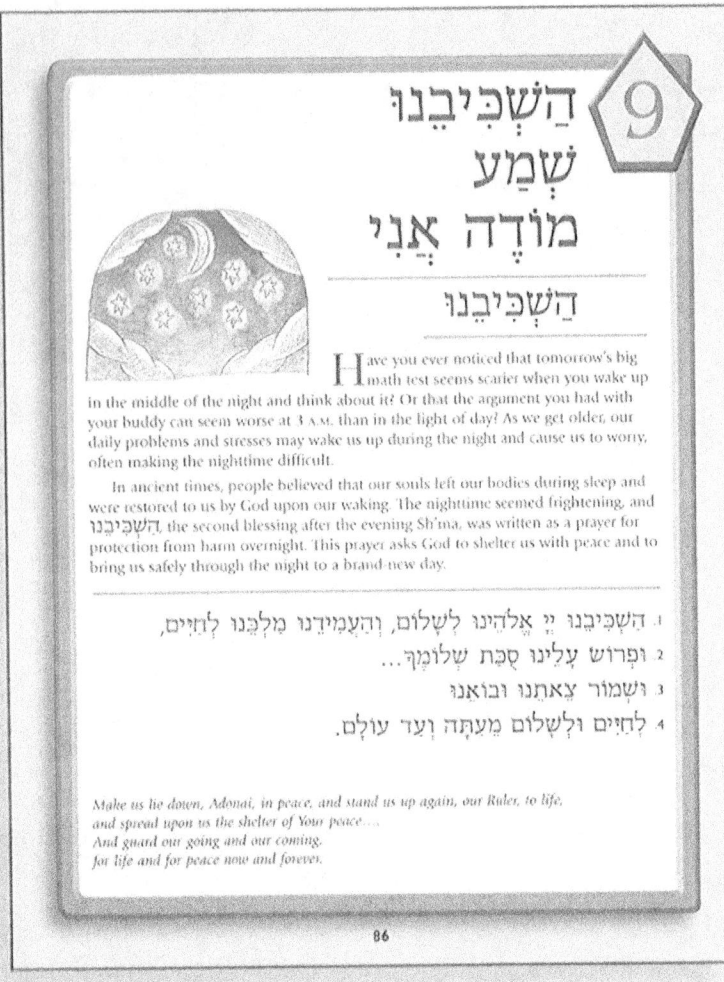

As a Family

You might wish to send home copies of "As a Family: Shelter of Peace" with the students at this time.

INTO THE TEXT

Direct students to the three prayer names at the top of the page.

Explain that these prayers are related to the cycle of night and day.

Call on students to read aloud the introduction to Hashkiveinu.

Note: The second evening blessing following the Sh'ma and V'ahavta is Hashkiveinu.

Call on students to read aloud the English translation of the prayer.

Ask them to explain the phrases "stand us up again" (*let us wake up again*), "shelter of Your peace" (*God's protection*), and "guard our going and our coming" (*we ask God to protect us when we leave our home and when we return*).

Reading Practice

Write the word שָׁלוֹם and the root שלמ on the chalkboard.

Explain that the root means more than "peace." It means "wholeness" or "completeness."

Discuss the connection between "peace" and "wholeness" or "completeness." (*when there is peace, life is whole; when there is strife, the world is incomplete*)

Ask the students to circle and read the three words meaning "peace" in lines 1, 2, and 4. (לְשָׁלוֹם, שְׁלוֹמֶךָ, וּלְשָׁלוֹם) Create fruit for these words and add them to the שלמ tree.

Reading Relay: Have one student read the first word on line 1. Have a second student read the first and second words on line 1. A third student reads the first, second, and third words on line 1. Continue building the reading in this way until the final student reads all four lines in the prayer.

An Interactive Relay: Prepare a paper baton for the relay. Each reader should pass the baton to the next reader as the relay progresses.

PRAYER DICTIONARY

Display Word Cards 93 and 94 to form the phrase סֻכַּת שְׁלוֹמֶךָ ("the shelter of Your peace").

Ask: What can we do to make our home a "shelter of peace." (*treat each other with respect; resolve disagreements amicably; share household chores; divide TV and computer time fairly; give everyone a chance to talk*)

Holiday Connection: Ask the students to describe a sukkah.

Ask them what the connection is between a "shelter of peace" and a sukkah. (*both cover and protect us; both suggest that security comes from faith in God, rather than from living in homes with locks on the doors*)

Display Word Cards 91 and 92.

Call two students to the front of the classroom. Have a third student be the reader. The reader should say the Hebrew word on either Word Card 91 or 92 and the two students should do what the word says, that is, lie down or stand up. Repeat several times with different students.

OPPOSITES ATTRACT

Complete the exercise together or allow students to complete it individually.

Make a fruit for the word וְהַעֲמִידֵנוּ and add it to the עמד tree.

Photo Op

Call on a student to read the caption.

Ask the students if they've ever seen a spectacular sunset. Where were they at the time?

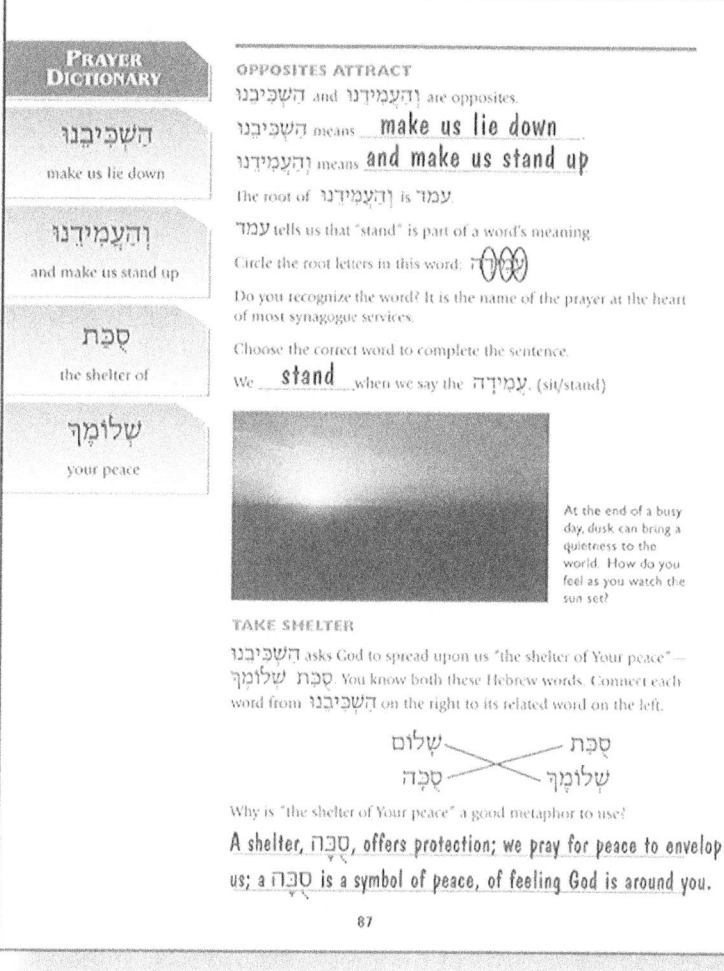

TAKE SHELTER

Allow the students several minutes to complete the activity. Encourage them to draw on previous class discussions to answer the question at the end. Have the students share their insights.

COMINGS AND GOINGS

Read aloud the paragraph with the students.

Direct them to complete the activity. Call on individuals to read the two lines aloud.

Direct students to page 86. Have them circle the two Hebrew words meaning "our going and our coming" in line 3. (צֵאתֵנוּ וּבוֹאֵנוּ)

Read page 86, lines 3–4, in unison with the students. Then read all four lines in unison.

THEME OF THE PRAYER

Allow the students time to respond. Call on individuals to share their responses with the class.

INTRODUCING שְׁמַע

Direct students to the introductory paragraphs at the top of the page.

Call on two students to each read a paragraph.

Ask the class for examples of simple, yet powerful, words or statements that need no explanation. ("*I love you*"; "*you're right*"; "*I'm sorry*"; "*I made a mistake*"; "*Will you marry me?*"; "*I forgive you*")

About the Prayer

The Sh'ma comes from the Torah (Deuteronomy 6:4). It is a statement of faith in and allegiance to God. In the prayer, we declare our belief in one God. The second line of the Sh'ma (בָּרוּךְ שֵׁם כְּבוֹד מַלְכוּתוֹ לְעוֹלָם וָעֶד) was first said in the ancient Temple in Jerusalem; it was the response given by the people after hearing the Divine Name pronounced by the High Priest. Later it became the response to the first line of the Sh'ma.

Traditionally, the second line is recited silently or in a soft voice, to distinguish it from the rest of the Sh'ma, which comes from the Torah.

Extending the Lesson

Encourage students to recite the Sh'ma each evening before going to sleep and each morning upon arising.

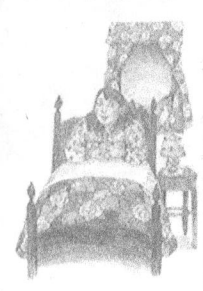

INTRODUCING מוֹדֶה אֲנִי

Ask the students what good things they anticipated when they woke up today. Is anyone looking forward to a special upcoming event?

Call on students to read aloud the introduction to Modeh Ani at the top of the page.

Ask: What do we thank God for when we recite Modeh Ani? (*symbolically returning our souls to us and giving us a new day to live*)

Choose a student to read the English translation of the prayer.

The Prayer Connection

Ask: What is the connection between Hashkiveinu and Modeh Ani?
(*Hashkiveinu: Asks for God's protection from harm overnight. In ancient times people thought their souls left their bodies during the night and were restored to them by God when they awoke in the morning. Modeh Ani: Thanks God for returning our souls.*)

Reading Practice

Call on a boy to read the first word in line 1 for boys and men. (מוֹדֶה)

Have all the boys read the first three words of their version in unison.

Call on a girl to read the first word in line 1 for girls and women. (מוֹדָה)

Have all the girls read the first three words of their version in unison.

Have the class read the prayer in unison with boys and girls reading their own versions.

Write the following vowels on the chalkboard:
יְ
ֶ ֵ

Ask what sound the vowels have. ("eh")

Call on individuals to read the words in the prayer that have the "eh" sound.
(מוֹדֶה, לְפָנֶיךָ, מֶלֶךְ, שֶׁהֶחֱזַרְתָּ, בְּחֶמְלָה, אֱמוּנָתֶךָ)

PRAYER DICTIONARY

Round 1

Display Words Cards 6 and 95–99 in random order facing the class.

Direct a student to read the first six words of the prayer on page 90, pausing after each word.

Direct another student to place the Word Cards in the correct right-to-left order as the first student reads each word.

Round 2

Place Word Cards 6 and 95–99 in random order with the English side facing the class.

Direct a student to read the first six Hebrew words of the prayer, pausing after each word.

Direct another student to select the matching English Word Cards while the first one reads, and place them in the correct left-to-right order.

Reinforcing Word Order

Use one of the Reinforcing Word Order techniques described at the front of this guide (page 7).

MATCH THE MEANING

Have students complete the exercise individually. Ask them to cover the Prayer Dictionary while they work and then to uncover it to check their answers.

Photo Op

Call on a student to read the caption.

Ask: What does the phrase "the potential in each new day" mean? (*the new and exciting things one can do that day; the ways in which we have the potential to shape events and to do good in the world*)

Encourage the students to recite Modeh Ani when they wake up in the morning and to think about the potential in the new day.

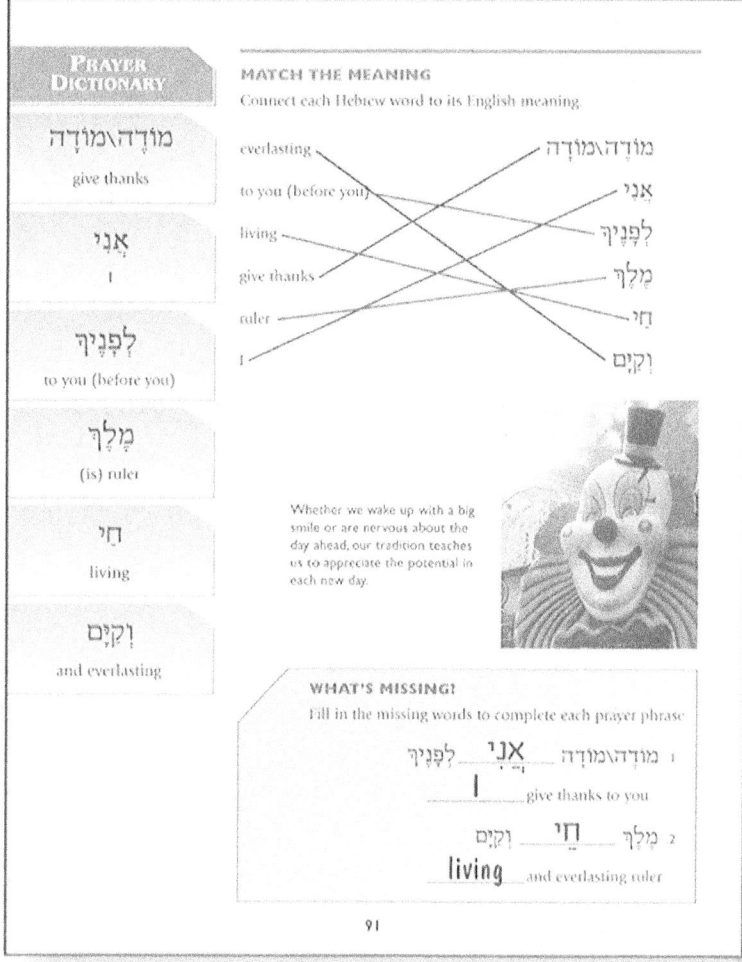

WHAT'S MISSING?

Display Word Cards 6 and 95–99 again with the Hebrew side facing the class.

Have students complete the exercise individually. Direct them to cover the Prayer Dictionary and to select the missing words from the Word Card display. They can then uncover the Prayer Dictionary to check their own work.

FROM THE SOURCES

Read the explanation aloud with the students. Have them read the citation as follows: Book of Lamentations, Chapter 3, Verses 22–23.

Direct the students to circle and read the same two words in the prayer on page 90. (רַבָּה אֱמוּנָתֶךָ)

Games…Games…Games

Select one or more games from the Classroom Games section at the front of this guide (pages 9–11), to reinforce reading and concepts in Modeh Ani.

WRITE YOUR OWN PRAYER

Call on a student to read aloud the introduction to the activity.

Before students begin writing their prayer for the new day, discuss words and themes they can use to express their feelings. (*family; thank you; grateful; God; love; peace; hope; healthy; life; new beginning*)

FLUENT READING

Play Tic-Tac-Toe with the prayer lines.

Draw a Tic-Tac-Toe grid on the chalkboard. Write nine line numbers—one in each of the nine boxes. Form two teams, X and O.

Decide which team should go first. A player on that team should select a box and read the complete line corresponding to the number in that box. If correct, the player should place the team's mark—X or O—in the box. It is then the second team's turn. Continue playing until one team gets three consecutive marks.

If a player reads incorrectly, the opposing team must recognize the error and correct it to write their team's mark in the grid.

You may wish to play the game again. This time write different numbers in the boxes and have the other team go first.

WORKSHEET

Duplicate and hand out copies of the worksheet for Lesson 9 to review skills and concepts.

FAMILY EDUCATION

Duplicate and send home copies of "As a Family: Shelter of Peace" (at the back of this guide) if you did not already do so.

FLUENT READING

Each line below contains a word you know. Practice reading the lines.

1. וַאֲנַחְנוּ כּוֹרְעִים וּמִשְׁתַּחֲוִים וּמוֹדִים לִפְנֵי מֶלֶךְ מַלְכֵי הַמְּלָכִים, הַקָּדוֹשׁ בָּרוּךְ הוּא.
2. שָׁמוֹר וְזָכוֹר בְּדִבּוּר אֶחָד הִשְׁמִיעָנוּ אֵל הַמְיֻחָד
3. בַּיּוֹם הַהוּא יִהְיֶה יְיָ אֶחָד וּשְׁמוֹ אֶחָד.
4. בָּרוּךְ אַתָּה, יְיָ אֱלֹהֵינוּ, מֶלֶךְ הָעוֹלָם, אֲשֶׁר קִדְּשָׁנוּ בְּמִצְוֹתָיו וְצִוָּנוּ לֵישֵׁב בַּסֻּכָּה.
5. הַפּוֹרֵשׂ סֻכַּת שָׁלוֹם עָלֵינוּ, וְעַל כָּל עַמּוֹ יִשְׂרָאֵל, וְעַל יְרוּשָׁלָיִם.
6. שְׁמַע! בַּיָּמִים הָהֵם בַּזְּמַן הַזֶּה.
7. שָׁלוֹם עֲלֵיכֶם, מַלְאֲכֵי הַשָּׁרֵת, מַלְאֲכֵי עֶלְיוֹן.
8. נוֹדֶה לְךָ וּנְסַפֵּר תְּהִלָּתֶךָ.
9. שָׁלוֹם רָב עַל יִשְׂרָאֵל עַמְּךָ תָּשִׂים לְעוֹלָם.
10. מוֹדִים אֲנַחְנוּ לָךְ, שָׁאַתָּה הוּא יְיָ אֱלֹהֵינוּ.

Shabbat Morning Service

PRELIMINARY PRAYERS

מוֹדֶה אֲנִי

THE SH'MA AND ITS BLESSINGS

בָּרְכוּ

יוֹצֵר אוֹר

אַהֲבָה רַבָּה

שְׁמַע

וְאָהַבְתָּ

מִי כָמֹכָה

THE SHABBAT AMIDAH

אָבוֹת

אָבוֹת וְאִמָּהוֹת

גְּבוּרוֹת

קְדוּשָּׁה

קְדוּשַּׁת הַיּוֹם

עֲבוֹדָה

הוֹדָאָה

שִׂים שָׁלוֹם

עֹשֶׂה שָׁלוֹם

SHABBAT MORNING SERVICE

Ask: What do you think the phrase "siddur geography" means? (*knowing the structure of the service; finding your place in the siddur; knowing where a prayer falls in the order of the service*)

Explain that the prayer chart on these pages represents the geography of the Shabbat morning service. Tell students the flow of the service—the Sh'ma and its blessings, then the Amidah, the Torah service, and the concluding prayers.

Give each student a siddur. Together, look through the siddurim to locate the different prayers in the chart.

Variation: Have students work in pairs or small groups to find the prayers in the siddur. Give students a sense of where to look, for example, in the Shabbat morning service between pages X and Y. Have students write down the page number next to the name of each prayer in their texts.

Prayer Mastery

Consider using the chart as a checklist to assess students' prayer mastery. Over the course of the last few weeks of the term, have students locate the prayers in the siddur and read them. When they read the prayer fluently—or you are satisfied with their reading—allow them to put a check mark or a star next to the name of the prayer in their texts.

Challenge: Ask students to explain the theme of each prayer, to earn an additional check or a different color star.

THE TORAH SERVICE

אֵין כָּמוֹךָ
אַב הָרַחֲמִים
כִּי מִצִּיּוֹן
לְךָ יְיָ
בִּרְכוֹת הַתּוֹרָה
וְזֹאת הַתּוֹרָה
בִּרְכוֹת הַהַפְטָרָה
עֵץ חַיִּים הִיא

ADDITIONAL PRAYERS

עָלֵינוּ
קַדִּישׁ
אֵין כֵּאלֹהֵינוּ

LESSON 9
Worksheet

Name: _____

הַשְׁכִּיבֵנוּ / שְׁמַע / מוֹדָה אֲנִי

1. Draw a line to connect each root to the matching English in each column.

choose	קדש	mercy, compassion	עשה
road, way	דרך	great	רחם
say	בחר	stand	עמד
holy	שלם	worship, work	גדל
peace	ברך	do, make	עבד
bless, praise	אמר	rule	מלך

2. Add the suffix נוּ to complete each word from הַשְׁכִּיבֵנוּ.

   וְהַעֲמִיד_____   אֱלֹהֵי_____   הַשְׁכִּיב_____

   וּבוֹא_____   צֵאת_____   עָלֵי_____   מַלְכֵּ_____

   What does נוּ mean? _____

   Explain the meaning of הַשְׁכִּיבֵנוּ in your own words.

   _____

3. Write the words of the שְׁמַע in the correct order on the line below.

   יְיָ   שְׁמַע   אֱלֹהֵינוּ   יְיָ   יִשְׂרָאֵל   אֶחָד

   _____

   Explain the meaning of the שְׁמַע in your own words.

   _____

4. Use the words below to complete the first part of מוֹדָה אֲנִי.

   לְפָנֶיךָ   חַי

   מוֹדֶה\מוֹדָה אֲנִי _____ מֶלֶךְ _____ וְקַיָּם

5. When do we say מוֹדָה אֲנִי? _____

6. What thought are we expressing in מוֹדָה אֲנִי? _____

HINENI—THE NEW HEBREW THROUGH PRAYER 3 © Behrman House Publishers

III. ENRICHMENT AND SUPPLEMENTARY MATERIALS

FAMILY EDUCATION

The Beginning

אֵין כָּמוֹךָ בָאֱלֹהִים, יְיָ, וְאֵין כְּמַעֲשֶׂיךָ.

Ein kamocha va'elohim, Adonai, v'ein k'ma'a'secha.

There is none like You, Adonai, among the gods (other people worship), and there are no deeds like Yours.

We begin the Torah service by praising God, not the Torah itself. By doing so, we acknowledge the traditional belief that the Torah comes from God. The Torah lists not only the mitzvot (commandments) by which we live Jewish lives, but also describes the great deeds that God performed for the people of Israel. We, too, may be able to identify great deeds—blessings—in our own lives.

Consider the blessings in *your* family's lives. On the lines below, have each family member list one or two things for which he or she is grateful. When you have completed your "blessing list," recite as a family the verse above in thanksgiving for your blessings.

As a Family

From Generation to Generation

בָּרוּךְ שֶׁנָּתַן תּוֹרָה לְעַמּוֹ יִשְׂרָאֵל בִּקְדֻשָּׁתוֹ.

Baruch shenatan Torah l'amo Yisra'el bik'dushato.

Praised is the One, who in holiness gave the Torah to God's people Israel.

The Torah links us with our ancestors and our descendants. From it we learn how our ancestors lived and the choices they made that affect us today. We pass the Torah on from one generation to the next, safeguarding it and its teachings.

Just as the Torah preserves the heritage of the Jewish people, so do our family heirlooms preserve our family's memories and traditions. List below the heirlooms that have been preserved in your family: photo albums, scrapbooks, jewelry, clothing, books, ritual objects, names, family customs. Write down ways in which each is significant to your family today. How does each one help to preserve your family memories and traditions?

Name: _____

Continuing the Tradition

בָּרוּךְ אַתָּה, יְיָ, נוֹתֵן הַתּוֹרָה.

Baruch atah, Adonai, notein hatorah.

Praised are You, Adonai, who gives us the Torah.

In this blessing, said before the Torah reading, we thank God for choosing us to receive the gift of Torah. Your child will say these words upon becoming Bar or Bat Mitzvah. In anticipation of the event, have your child interview a family member or friend who became Bar or Bat Mitzvah ten or more years ago. Together they can reflect on the rich tradition that has been passed on from one generation to the next.

- What is your Hebrew name? _____
- When did you become Bar or Bat Mitzvah? _____
- How was it different for boys and for girls? _____
- Describe some of the rituals you followed (chanting from the Torah, giving a *d'var Torah* [interpretation of the Torah portion], leading the service).

_____

_____

- With whom did you celebrate? _____

_____

_____

- What special memories do you carry with you from that day? _____

_____

_____

HINENI—THE NEW HEBREW THROUGH PRAYER 3 © Behrman House Publishers
www.behrmanhouse.com/family

As a Family

Name: _____

Telling the Truth

בָּרוּךְ אַתָּה יְיָ, הַבּוֹחֵר בַּתּוֹרָה...וּבִנְבִיאֵי הָאֱמֶת וָצֶדֶק.

Baruch atah Adonai, haboher batorah…uvin'vi'ei ha'emet vatzedek.

Praised are You, Adonai, the One who takes delight in (chooses) the Torah…
and in prophets of truth and righteousness (justice).

A child becoming Bar or Bat Mitzvah may read from one of the books of the prophets, called the haftarah ("conclusion"). The selection above is part of the blessing said before the haftarah reading. The prophets were called "prophets of truth and righteousness" because they spoke about righteous behavior to the Jewish people.

Telling the truth—אֱמֶת—is an important mitzvah. Psalm 15 teaches us that only those who "speak truth in their hearts and have no slander on their tongues" will "live in God's house." But very few of us have never told a lie. As a family, discuss the question below and write the response of each family member.

Is it ever acceptable to tell a lie? If not, explain why. If you think it is, give an example of such a circumstance.

Family member: _____

Response: _____

_____

Family member: _____

Response: _____

_____

Family member: _____

Response: _____

_____

As a Family

Roots and Branches

עֵץ חַיִּים הִיא לַמַּחֲזִיקִים בָּהּ, וְתֹמְכֶיהָ מְאֻשָּׁר.

Eitz hayyim hi lamahazikim bah, v'tomchehah m'ushar.

It (the Torah) is a tree of life to those who uphold it,
and those who support it are happy.

When we return the Torah to the Ark, we sing a prayer comparing the Torah to a tree of life—עֵץ חַיִּים הִיא (Eitz Hayyim Hi). Just as a tree is a living thing, with roots that reach down into the earth and branches that reach up to the sun, so too is the Torah a living thing. Like a tree, it has roots that reach back to our ancestors. And like a tree, it has branches that will reach out to generations that will continue to read it and believe in its teachings.

Tell us on the lines below how previous generations in your family have strengthened the roots and extended the branches of your own family tree. For example, what have you learned from your grandparents and great-grandparents? How have they influenced your family's values?

_____
_____
_____
_____
_____
_____

HINENI—THE NEW HEBREW THROUGH PRAYER 3 © Behrman House Publishers
www.behrmanhouse.com/family

Name: _____

Showing Respect for God

וַאֲנַחְנוּ כּוֹרְעִים וּמִשְׁתַּחֲוִים וּמוֹדִים

Va'anahnu kor'im umishtahavim umodim

And we bend the knee, bow, and give thanks

We enact the words of עָלֵינוּ (Aleinu) and show our respect for God when we bow during the prayer. Bowing is just one way we can show our respect for God. As a family, discuss other ways to show respect and honor for God. Include but do not limit yourself to ritual observance, such as praying and lighting candles. Are there ways you can honor God by serving other people? Write your thoughts below.

_____

_____

_____

_____

_____

_____

In Memory

יְהֵא שְׁמֵהּ רַבָּה מְבָרַךְ לְעָלַם וּלְעָלְמֵי עָלְמַיָּא.

Y'hei sh'mei rabah m'varach l'alam ul'almei almaya.

May God's great name be blessed forever and ever.

Surprisingly, the Mourner's Kaddish, said in memory of those who have died, doesn't mention death at all. Instead, it praises God and expresses hope and promise for the future. We can remember our loved ones through stories told and retold, photographs and keepsakes, perhaps even videos. As a family, look around the house for cherished items that represent loved ones who are no longer with you. Choose one or two and explain their significance to your family on the lines below.

_____

_____

_____

_____

_____

_____

As a Family

The Roles We Play

אֵין כֵּאלֹהֵינוּ, אֵין כַּאדוֹנֵינוּ, אֵין כְּמַלְכֵּנוּ, אֵין כְּמוֹשִׁיעֵנוּ.

Ein keiloheinu, Ein kadoneinu, Ein k'malkeinu, Ein k'moshi'einu.

There is none like our God, There is none like our Sovereign,
There is none like our Ruler, There is none like our Savior.

The joyful hymn that we sing at the conclusion of Shabbat and holiday services, אֵין כֵּאלֹהֵינוּ (Ein Keloheinu), praises God and celebrates God's uniqueness. The prayer lists some of God's different roles—Sovereign, Ruler, and Savior. Each role reflects unique aspects of the relationship between the Jewish people and God.

In our own families, too, each person plays different roles. Write each family member's name below. Then list the roles that person plays in the lives of others (for example, Susan: daughter, granddaughter, girl scout, student, member of the swim team, youth group leader, friend). Discuss how those roles reflect different aspects of the person.

HINENI—THE NEW HEBREW THROUGH PRAYER 3 © Behrman House Publishers
www.behrmanhouse.com/family

Name: _____

Shelter of Peace

וּפְרוֹשׁ עָלֵינוּ סֻכַּת שְׁלוֹמֶךָ...

Ufros aleinu sukkat shlomecha...

And spread upon us the shelter of Your peace...

הַשְׁכִּיבֵנוּ (Hashkiveinu) is a blessing recited during the evening service. The line above is from the version recited on Shabbat. הַשְׁכִּיבֵנוּ was written as a prayer for protection from harm overnight, since in ancient times people believed that our souls leave our bodies during sleep and are restored by God upon our waking. הַשְׁכִּיבֵנוּ asks God to shelter us with peace during the dark of night and to bring us safely to a brand new day.

Talk about the ways your family creates a feeling of security and protection as darkness approaches. Do your children have favorite blankets or toys to take to bed? Do you have family "talk time"? List the ways your family builds a "shelter of peace" in your home as night approaches.

_____
_____
_____
_____
_____
_____

TECHNIQUES FOR USE WITH SPECIAL NEEDS STUDENTS

Like most classes, yours probably includes a diverse group of students with different learning styles and needs, who achieve mastery at different rates. The variety of activities in *Hineni* offers your students a broad selection of learning opportunities that can be easily modified for students with special learning needs.

Without practice, students frequently lose some of their Hebrew decoding skills over the summer. This is particularly true of students with special learning needs. It is helpful to assess such students' decoding skill levels individually at the very beginning of the new school year and review the letters and vowels with them.

It is important to use a diagnostic-prescriptive approach. By noting students' decoding errors, you can identify their needs, reteach problematic letters and vowels, and provide the necessary practice to bring the students back up to speed. Use your school's primer to reteach basic reading skills. Retest the students to be certain that they have mastered the troublesome items.

Here are some teaching tips that can help you work more effectively with special needs students.

- Be ready to assist the students in decoding new words and phrases. Model the correct pronunciation and phrasing before they read any segment of the book. Do not let them struggle. Reinforce word attack skills by breaking words into syllables. Repeat words and phrases several times, and do not assume that all your students will be able to read them fluently and accurately when they see the same words and phrases again later.

- Students with significant learning difficulties may have trouble keeping up with the class. Prioritize your goals for them. Identify the core elements of the text that you want them to master; this will help them keep up with the rest of the class. Allow extra time for them to finish an assignment, or reduce the number of items they are expected to complete. Offer them other modes of responding, for example, orally instead of in writing, underlining or circling instead of copying, or working together with an aide or a buddy.

- Although the Hebrew text in *Hineni* has separated and numbered lines, some students may benefit from using an index card or pencil to help track across the line. In some instances, masking the rest of the page to reduce distractions can enable them to read more easily.

- Some students, especially those who are shy, lack confidence, or have learning differences, are reluctant to read aloud in class. You can provide an alternative method of monitoring their reading progress by listening to small groups while the rest of the class is working on the other sections of the lesson. This is also a more efficient use of class time.

- For students who require additional support in order to achieve mastery, enlist parents as partners in the educational process. Short periods of daily practice with an audiotape at home will help the students retain what they have learned in class and build toward fluency and accuracy. Parents can "sign off" on the practice schedule even if they themselves do not feel that they are competent Hebrew readers.

By adapting your teaching techniques to meet the individual learning styles and special needs of your students, you can help every member of your class master the skills in this book.

ANSWERS TO WORKSHEETS

LESSON 1 Worksheet

Name: _____

אֵת פְּתַח הַדְּבָרִים

1. Complete the prayer sentence below by filling in the Hebrew words in the order in which they appear in the prayer. יִמְלֹךְ יְהֹוָה מֶלֶךְ יְהֹוָה מָלָךְ יְהֹוָה

   יְהֹוָה _מָלָךְ_ יְהֹוָה _מֶלֶךְ_ יְהֹוָה _יִמְלֹךְ_ לְעוֹלָם וָעֶד.

   Adonai is _Ruler_, Adonai _ruled_, Adonai will rule forever and ever.

   What is the root of the three Hebrew words you wrote? _מ_ _ל_ _ך_

2. Write the root of each Hebrew word on the first line below it. (Note: Sometimes a root letter doesn't appear in a word.) Then write the English equivalent of the root on the second line.

הַנִּלְכָּה	בְּרַחֲמָיו	רַחֲמִים	עֹשֶׂה
מלך	רחם	רחם	עשה
rule	mercy, compassion	mercy, compassion	do, make

3. Add the suffix ךָ to complete each word.

   _שִׁמְךָ_ _אֱלֹהֶיךָ_ _בְּךָ_

   What does the suffix ךָ mean? _your_ _you_

4. Read the following line from אֵת פְּתַח, then answer the questions that follow.

   אָב הָרַחֲמָן הֵיטִיבָה בִרְצוֹנְךָ אֶת צִיּוֹן תִּבְנֶה חוֹמוֹת יְרוּשָׁלָיִם

   Which Hebrew word means "father" or "parent"? _אָב_
   Write the word for "Jerusalem." _יְרוּשָׁלָיִם_
   Which word is another name for Jerusalem? _צִיּוֹן_

5. The Torah service has three main parts. Fill in the missing parts on the blank lines below.
   1. Taking the Torah out of the Ark
   2. Reading the Torah
   3. Returning the Torah to the Ark

LESSON 2 Worksheet

Name: _____

כִּי מִצִיּוֹן / לְךָ יְיָ

1. Write the English meaning below each Hebrew word.

הַתּוֹרָה	יִשְׂרָאֵל	מִירוּשָׁלָיִם	צִיּוֹן
Torah	Israel	Jerusalem	Zion

2. Unscramble the first sentence of כִּי מִצִיּוֹן and write the words in the correct order.

   תֵצֵא יְיָ כִּי דְבַר מִירוּשָׁלָיִם תוֹרָה וּ מִצִיּוֹן

   כִּי מִצִיּוֹן תֵּצֵא תוֹרָה וּדְבַר יְיָ מִירוּשָׁלָיִם

3. Why do we carry the Torah up and down the aisles of the congregation before the Torah reading?
   to bring us closer to the Torah so we can touch it with a siddur or tallit; to show that the Torah belongs to the Jewish people; to build anticipation; so we can show respect for the Torah

4. Connect the root to the matching English.

   speak — דבר
   holy — קדש
   make — עשה
   mercy — רחם
   rule — מלך

5. Name the three days of the week on which the Torah is read.
   Monday _Thursday_ _Shabbat_

6. Explain how Ezra the scribe helped perpetuate the tradition of reading Torah.
   Ezra wanted to rebuild Jewish life in Israel after the Jews' return from exile in Babylonia. He began by reading from the Torah. Ezra knew the people had to hear Torah often if they were to live by its laws, so he read Torah three days each week—on Mondays and Thursdays (the two market days in ancient times), and on Shabbat. The Torah was also read aloud on festival days.

LESSON 3 Worksheet

Name: _____

בִּרְכוֹת הַתּוֹרָה

1. What is the name of the first part of the blessing before the Torah reading? Choose your answer from the words below.

   בָּרְכוּ

   שְׁמַע   בָּרוּךְ   עוֹלָם

2. Why does this prayer introduce the blessing before the Torah reading?

   Like the Call to Worship, this prayer calls the people to read Torah and to praise God.

3. The following phrases are part of the blessing before the Torah reading. Number them in the correct order, using the English translation below as your guide.

   אֶת הַתּוֹרָה [4]   מִבָּל הָעַמִּים [2]
   אֲשֶׁר בָּחַר [1]   וְנָתַן לָנוּ [3]

   for choosing us from all the nations and giving us God's Torah

4. The following phrases are part of the blessing after the Torah reading. Number them in the correct order, using the English translation below as your guide.

   אֲשֶׁר נָתַן לָנוּ [1]   וְחַיֵּי עוֹלָם [3]
   תּוֹרַת אֱמֶת [2]   נָטַע בְּתוֹכֵנוּ [4]

   who gave us the Torah of truth, and implanted within us eternal life

5. Explain the meaning of these Torah terms.

   going up to the Torah to recite the blessings; going up to live in Israel — עֲלִיָּה

   Torah portion (there are 54) — פָּרָשָׁה

   Torah reader (masc/fem) — בַּעַל קוֹרֵא/בַּעֲלַת קוֹרֵא

   a blessing asking God to protect us with good health and for the recovery of those who are ill; a blessing given to one receiving an aliyah — מִי שֶׁבֵּרַךְ

6. On which holiday do we finish reading the Torah and begin all over again?

   Simḥat Torah

LESSON 4 Worksheet

Name: _____

בִּרְכוֹת הַהַפְטָרָה

1. How many blessings are chanted *before* the haftarah reading? __1__
   How many blessings are chanted *after* the haftarah reading? __4__

2. Find the English meaning of the word בִּרְכוֹת by unscrambling the following letters: ncoionscul. Write your answer on the line. __conclusion__

3. Write the English meaning on the line next to each Hebrew word below.

   Writings — כְּתוּבִים   Prophets — נְבִיאִים   Torah — תּוֹרָה

4. Lightly circle the first letter in each Hebrew word in Question 3. Use the circled letters to help you answer the following:

   תנ״ך is the name of the Hebrew Bible. How did the Hebrew Bible get its name?

   The name is made up of the first letter in the name of each part of the Bible.

   In which section of the תנ״ך do we find the haftarah readings? __נְבִיאִים__

5. Write the number of each English word below next to its matching Hebrew root.

   1. compassion   2. holy   3. speak   4. bless, praise   5. choose   6. say

   אמר __6__   דבר __3__   ברך __5__
   בחר __4__   קדש __1__   רחם __2__

6. Write the number of each English word below next to the matching Hebrew word.

   1. righteousness, justice   2. truth   3. prophet   4. Israel
   5. Moses   6. God's people

   עַמּוֹ __6__   צֶדֶק __1__   אֱמֶת __2__
   מֹשֶׁה __5__   נָבִיא __3__   יִשְׂרָאֵל __4__

7. Name two qualities the prophets were required to have __righteousness, honesty, faithfulness, justness__

LESSON 5 Worksheet

Name: _____

עַל שְׁלֹשָׁה דְבָרִים / עֵץ חַיִּים הִיא / וְזֹאת הַתּוֹרָה

1. Number the English and Hebrew phrases in the correct order of וְזֹאת הַתּוֹרָה.

   _5_ through Moses   אֲשֶׁר שָׂם מֹשֶׁה _2_
   _1_ and this is the Torah וְזֹאת הַתּוֹרָה _4_
   _3_ before the people of Israel עַל פִּי יְיָ _1_
   _4_ by the word of Adonai לִפְנֵי בְּנֵי יִשְׂרָאֵל _5_
   _2_ that Moses placed   בְּיַד מֹשֶׁה _3_

   Write the Hebrew word for "Moses." _____
   Write the Hebrew word for "Israel." _____

2. Explain each Torah term below.
   hagbahah __the honor of lifting the Torah for the congregation to see the words on the scroll__
   g'lilah __the honor of rolling and dressing the Torah__

3. What is the meaning of the phrase עֵץ חַיִּים? __Tree of Life__
   Explain in your own words why the Torah is called עֵץ חַיִּים.
   __The Torah gives life to the Jewish people. It nourishes them. Just as the roots of a tree__
   __secure it in the ground, so do the roots of Torah keep the Jewish people secure.__

4. Using the following Hebrew words, fill in the missing words and phrases in the prayer below.

   עַל שְׁלֹשָׁה דְבָרִים הָעוֹלָם עוֹמֵד עַל הַתּוֹרָה וְעַל הָעֲבוֹדָה וְעַל גְּמִילוּת חֲסָדִים

   __The world stands on three things:__ _____ on Torah
   _____ on worship
   and on acts of loving-kindness.

5. Explain each of the following terms and give an example.
   humash: __service to God. Examples: lighting Shabbat candles, reciting Kiddush, praying in synagogue__
   Torah: __Five Books of Moses; mitzvot; studying Torah; learning how to worship God__
   __and how to be a good person.__
   worship: __service to God. Examples: lighting Shabbat candles, reciting Kiddush, praying in synagogue__
   acts of loving-kindness: __good deeds; acts of kindness. Examples: giving tzedakah, visiting the sick,__
   __protecting the environment, respecting older people, behaving with derech eretz__

LESSON 6 Worksheet

Name: _____

עָלֵינוּ

1. Write the English meaning on the line next to each Hebrew word or phrase below.

   __Ruler of rulers__ מַלְכֵי הַמְּלָכִים __to praise__ לְשַׁבֵּחַ
   __it is our duty__ עָלֵינוּ   __and we__ וַאֲנַחְנוּ
   __and thank__ לְהוֹדוֹת   __God__ אֱלֹהִים

2. The English phrases below are in the same order as in עָלֵינוּ. The Hebrew phrases are mixed up. Indicate the correct order of the Hebrew phrases by writing the number of the matching English next to each.

   (1) It is our duty to praise the God of all.
   (2) and we bend the knee, bow, and give thanks
   (3) before the Ruler of rulers
   (4) On that day God will be One and God's name will be One.

   וַאֲנַחְנוּ כּוֹרְעִים וּמִשְׁתַּחֲוִים וּמוֹדִים _2_
   לִפְנֵי מֶלֶךְ מַלְכֵי הַמְּלָכִים _3_
   בַּיּוֹם הַהוּא יִהְיֶה יְיָ אֶחָד וּשְׁמוֹ אֶחָד _4_
   עָלֵינוּ לְשַׁבֵּחַ לַאֲדוֹן הַכֹּל _1_

3. Why do we bend our knees and bow during עָלֵינוּ?
   __We act out the words of the prayer; we show respect and honor for God.__

4. Why is עָלֵינוּ a "pledge of loyalty" to God?
   __We declare our faithfulness to God; we praise God.__

LESSON 7 Worksheet

Name: _____

קָדוֹשׁ

1. What is the root of the word קָדוֹשׁ? ק ד שׁ
   Write the English equivalent of the root. __holy__

2. In what language is most of the קָדוֹשׁ written? __Aramaic__

3. The קָדוֹשׁ ends with a short Hebrew prayer. Circle the name of the prayer from the choices below.

   בָּרְכוּ (עֹשֶׂה שָׁלוֹם) שְׁמַע כִּי מִכָּבוֹד יָהּ

4. Below are words from the קָדוֹשׁ. In the right column, write each word next to its root. In the left column, write the English equivalent of the root.

English	Root	Word
rule	מלך	מַלְכוּתֵהּ
peace	שׁלם	שְׁלָמָא
holy	קדשׁ	קֻדְשָׁא
bless, praise	ברך	הַבְרָךְ
great	גדל	דְּגֻלַּת

5. Fill in the missing word in each sentence below.
   • The קָדוֹשׁ is recited only in the presence of ten Jewish adults, called a __minyan__
   • We say the קָדוֹשׁ in memory of __those who have died; loved ones who have died; those who died in the Holocaust__
   • The קָדוֹשׁ is a prayer of __praise__ to God.
   • The קָדוֹשׁ ends on an optimistic note. It ends with a wish for __peace__

6. Why do you think the Kaddish is recited by mourners even though it does not mention death?
   __We praise God even when we are sad; we take comfort from God; at our saddest moments, we speak words of promise and hope.__

LESSON 8 Worksheet

Name: _____

אֵין כֵּאלֹהֵינוּ

1. What is the meaning of the suffix נוּ in the following words? __us; our__
   אֱלֹהֵינוּ   מַלְכֵּנוּ   אֲדוֹנֵינוּ   מוֹשִׁיעֵנוּ
   Which of these words has the root "rule"? Write it here. __מַלְכֵּנוּ__

2. Write the number of the English phrase next to the matching Hebrew.
   (1) there is none   אֵין כְּ __2__
   (2) who is   מִי __5__
   (3) we will give thanks אֵין __1__
   (4) blessed is   נוֹדֶה __4__
   (5) you are   אַתָּה __3__

3. Circle the prefix in each Hebrew word below. Then draw a line to connect the prefix to its English meaning in the phrase below it.

   לַאדוֹנֵינוּ   (כַּאדוֹנֵינוּ)   (בֵּאלֹהֵינוּ)
   to our Ruler   like our Sovereign   like our God

4. The English phrases below are in the same order as in אֵין כֵּאלֹהֵינוּ. The Hebrew phrases are mixed up. Indicate the correct order of the Hebrew phrases by writing the number of the matching English next to each.

   1. There is none like our God.   2. There is none like our Sovereign.
   3. There is none like our Ruler. 4. There is none like our Savior.

   מִי כֵאלֹהֵינוּ __2__   מִי כְמַלְכֵּנוּ __4__
   נוֹדֶה לֵאלֹהֵינוּ __3__   בָּרוּךְ אֱלֹהֵינוּ __1__

5. Explain the theme of אֵין כֵּאלֹהֵינוּ in your own words. __God is unique; there is none like our God; we honor God in four ways—as our God, our Sovereign, our Ruler, and our Savior.__

LESSON 9
Worksheet

Name: _____

מוֹדֶה אֲנִי / שְׁמַע / וְאָהַבְתָּ

1. Draw a line to connect each root to the matching English in each column.

choose	קדשׁ	mercy, compassion	שׁמע
road, way	דרך	great	הדר
say	בחר	stand	עמד
holy	שׁלם	worship, work	גדל
peace	ברך	do, make	עבד
bless, praise	אמר	rule	מלך

2. Add the suffix נוּ to complete each word from וְאָהַבְתָּ.

   הֵגֵן נוּ   אֶת נוּ   אֱלֹהֵי נוּ   הַשְׁכִּיבֵ נוּ

   What does נוּ mean? __us; our__

   Explain the meaning of הַשְׁכִּיבֵנוּ in your own words.
   __asks God to protect us at night; asks God to shelter us with peace__

3. Write the words of the שְׁמַע in the correct order on the line below.

   אֶחָד יִשְׂרָאֵל יְיָ אֱלֹהֵינוּ שְׁמַע יְיָ

   __שְׁמַע יִשְׂרָאֵל יְיָ אֱלֹהֵינוּ יְיָ אֶחָד__

   Explain the meaning of the שְׁמַע in your own words.
   __There is only one God; God is unique; we express our loyalty to God.__

4. Use the words below to complete the first part of מוֹדֶה אֲנִי.

   יְיָ לְפָנֶיךָ

   __מוֹדֶה__ __אֲנִי__ __לְפָנֶיךָ__ __יְיָ__

5. When do we say מוֹדֶה אֲנִי? __when we wake up in the morning__

6. What thoughts are we expressing in מוֹדֶה אֲנִי? __thanking God for returning our souls to us and for giving us a new day__

PRAYER DICTIONARY

will be	יִהְיֶה	**י**	our sovereign	אֲדוֹנֵינוּ	**א**
will rule	יִמְלֹךְ		(there is) none	אֵין	
Jerusalem	יְרוּשָׁלַיִם		there is none like	אֵין כְּ	
Israel	יִשְׂרָאֵל		our God	אֱלֹהֵינוּ	
will be great	יִתְגַּדַּל		truth	אֱמֶת	
			I	אֲנִי	
			you are	אַתָּה הוּא	
like you	כָּמוֹךָ	**כ**	in truth	בֶּאֱמֶת	**ב**
(like) your deeds	(כְּ)מַעֲשֶׂיךָ		chose	בָּחַר	
			we trust(ed)	בָּטַחְנוּ	
God	(לְ)אָדוֹן	**ל**	on that day	בַּיּוֹם הַהוּא	
to us	לָנוּ		prophets	(בִּ)נְבִיאִים	
forever	לְעוֹלָם		us	בָּנוּ	
to God's people	לְעַמּוֹ		people of	בְּנֵי	
before	לִפְנֵי		in the world	בְּעָלְמָא	
to you (before you)	לְפָנֶיךָ		in God's holiness	בִּקְדֻשָּׁתוֹ	
to praise	לְשַׁבֵּחַ		blessed	בָּרִיךְ	
			blessing	בִּרְכָתָא	
happy	מְאֻשָּׁר	**מ**	acts of loving-kindness	גְּמִילוּת חֲסָדִים	**ג**
give thanks	מוֹדֶה וּמוֹדָה				
our savior	מוֹשִׁיעֵנוּ		things	דְּבָרִים	**ד**
who is like	מִי כְּ		ways of	דַּרְכֵי	
from Jerusalem	מִירוּשָׁלַיִם		its ways	דְּרָכֶיהָ	
from all	מִכָּל				
ruled	מָלַךְ		the land	הָאָרֶץ	**ה**
(is) ruler	מֶלֶךְ		the one who chooses	הַבּוֹחֵר	
Ruler of rulers	מֶלֶךְ מַלְכֵי הַמְּלָכִים		of all	הַכֹּל	
God's kingdom	מַלְכוּתֹה		spoken	הָאֲמוּרִים	
your sovereignty	מַלְכוּתְךָ		the worship	הָעֲבוֹדָה	
our ruler	מַלְכֵּנוּ		the world	הָעוֹלָם	
from Zion	מִצִּיּוֹן		the nations	הָעַמִּים	
Moses	מֹשֶׁה		merciful, the mercy	הָרַחֲמִים	
			make us lie down	הַשְׁכִּיבֵנוּ	
we will give thanks to	נוֹדֶה לְ	**נ**	the Torah	הַתּוֹרָה	
gives	נוֹתֵן				
pleasantness	נֹעַם		and we	וַאֲנַחְנוּ	**ו**
			and in the life of	וּבְחַיֵּי	
the shelter of	סֻכַּת	**ס**	and the word of	וּדְבַר	
			and make us stand up	וְהַעֲמִידֵנוּ	
God's servant	עַבְדּוֹ	**ע**	and this is	וְזֹאת	
eternal, world	עוֹלָם		and life (of)	וְחַיֵּי	
stands	עוֹמֵד		and will rule	וְיִמְלֹךְ	
on	עַל		and will be praised	וְיִשְׁתַּבַּח	
it is our duty	עָלֵינוּ		and will be holy	וְיִתְקַדַּשׁ	
God's people	עַמּוֹ		and thank	וּמוֹדִים	
tree	עֵץ		and your reign	וּמֶמְשַׁלְתְּךָ	
			and gave (and giving)	וְנָתַן	
holy	קָדִישׁ	**ק**	and righteousness (justice)	וְצֶדֶק	
			and everlasting	וְקַיָּם	
peace	שָׁלוֹם	**ש**			
your peace	שְׁלוֹמֶךָ		living	חַי	**ח**
peace	שְׁלָמָא		(of) life	חַיִּים	
three	שְׁלֹשָׁה				
placed, put	שָׂם		good (faithful)	טוֹבִים	**ט**
God's name	שְׁמֵהּ				
who gave	שֶׁנָּתַן				
Torah, teaching	תּוֹרָה	**ת**			
Torah of	תּוֹרַת				
God's Torah	תּוֹרָתוֹ				

WRITING CHART

Script	Print	Name	Letter
		Final Mem	ם
		Nun	נ
		Final Nun	ן
		Samech	ס
		Ayin	ע
		Pay	פּ
		Fay	פ
		Final Fay	ף
		Tsadee	צ
		Final Tsadee	ץ
		Koof	ק
		Resh	ר
		Shin	שׁ
		Sin	שׂ
		Tav	תּ
		Tav	ת

Script	Print	Name	Letter
		Alef	א
		Bet	בּ
		Vet	ב
		Gimmel	ג
		Dalet	ד
		Hay	ה
		Vav	ו
		Zayin	ז
		Het	ח
		Tet	ט
		Yud	י
		Kaf	כּ
		Chaf	כ
		Final Chaf	ך
		Lamed	ל
		Mem	מ

NOTES